HOW TO DEFEND YOURSELF

Effective & Practical
Techniques and Strategies
from Traditional Chinese Martial Arts

YMAA Publication Center
38 Hyde Park Avenue
Jamaica Plain, Massachusetts, 02130

First Edition Copyright © 1992 Yang's Martial Arts Association (YMAA)
Second Edition Copyright © 1996 by Yang, Jwing-Ming

10 9 8 7 6 5 4

Publisher's Cataloging in Publication
(Prepared by Quality Books Inc.)

Yang, Jwing-Ming, 1946-
    How to defend yourself: effective & practical martial arts
strategies/ by Yang Jwing-Ming— 2nd ed.
    p. cm.
    Preassigned LCCN: 95-61981.
    ISBN: 1-886969-34-5

    1. Self defense- Handbooks, manuals, etc. 2. Martial arts-
Handbooks, manuals, etc.   I. Title.

GV1111.Y3 1996   613.66
                                        QBI95-2696

Disclaimer:
The author and publisher of this material are NOT RESPONSIBLE in any
manner whatsoever for any injury which may occur through reading or following the instructions in this manual.
The activities, physical or otherwise, described in this material may be too
strenuous or dangerous for some people, and the reader(s) should consult a
physician before engaging in them.

Printed in USA

ACKNOWLEDGEMENTS

Thanks to A. Reza Farman-Farmaian for the photography, Wu, Wen-Ching for the drawings, and Michael Wiederhold for the typesetting. Thanks also to Ramel Rones, Jenifer Menefee, Rosemarie Clifford, Jay Landry, Carol Shearer-Best, and James Yang for general help; to David Ripianzi, James O'Leary, Jeffrey Pratt, Roger Whidden Jr., Dr. Thomas G. Gutheil, and many other YMAA members for proofing the manuscript and contributing many valuable suggestions and discussions. Special thanks to Alan Dougall for his editing. Again, deepest appreciation to Dr. Thomas G. Gutheil for his continued support.

A NOTE ON ENGLISH SPELLINGS OF CHINESE WORDS

YMAA Publication Center uses the Pinyin romanization system of Chinese to English. Pinyin is standard in the People's Republic of China, and in several world organizations, including the United Nations. Pinyin is also used in contemporary scholarship and journalism. Pinyin, which was introduced in China in the 1950's, replaces the older Wade-Giles and Yale systems.

Some common conversions:

Wade-Giles	Pinyin
Chi	Qi
Chi Kung	Qigong
Chin Na	Qin Na
Ching	Qing
Kung fu	Gongfu
Tai Chi Chuan	Taijiquan

For more complete conversion tables, please refer to the *People's Republic of China: Administrative Atlas, The Reform of the Chinese Written Language,* or a contemporary manual of style.

ABOUT THE AUTHOR

Dr. Yang, Jwing-Ming was born on August 11th, 1946, in Xinzhu Xian, Taiwan, Republic of China. He started his Wushu (Gongfu or Kung Fu) training at the age of fifteen under Shaolin White Crane (Bai He) Master Cheng, Gin-Gsao. Master Cheng originally learned Taizuquan from his grandfather when he was a child. When Master Cheng was fifteen years old, he started learning White Crane from Master Jin, Shao-Feng, and he followed him for twenty-three years until Master Jin's death.

In thirteen years of study (1961-1974) under Master Cheng, Dr. Yang became an expert in the White Crane style of Chinese martial arts, which includes both barehand techniques and the use of such weapons as saber, staff, spear, trident, two short rods, and many others. With the same master he also studied White Crane Qin Na (Chin Na), Tui Na and Dian Xue massages, and herbal treatment.

At the age of sixteen, Dr. Yang began the study of Taijiquan (Yang Style) under Master Kao Tao. After learning from Master Kao, Dr. Yang continued his study and research of Taijiquan with several masters and senior practitioners such as Master Li, Mao-Ching and Mr. Wilson Chen in Taipei. Master Li learned his Taijiquan from the well-known Master Han, Ching-Tan, and Mr. Chen learned his Taijiquan from Master Chang, Xiang-San. Dr. Yang has mastered the Taiji barehand sequence, pushing hands, the two-person fighting sequence, Taiji sword, Taiji saber, and Taiji Qigong.

When Dr. Yang was eighteen years old he entered Tamkang College in Taipei Xian to study Physics. In college he began the study of traditional Shaolin Long Fist (Changquan or Chang Chuan) with Master Li, Mao-Ching at the Tamkang College Goushu Club (1964-1968), and eventually became an assistant instructor under Master Li. In 1971 he completed his M.S. degree in Physics at the National Taiwan University, and then served in the Chinese Air Force from 1971 to 1972. In the service, Dr. Yang taught Physics at the Junior Academy of the Chinese Air Force while also teaching Wushu. After being honorably discharged in 1972, he returned to Tamkang College to teach Physics and resume study under Master Li. From Master Li, Dr. Yang learned Northern style Wushu, which includes both barehand (especially kicking) techniques and numerous weapons.

In 1974 Dr. Yang came to the United States to study Mechanical Engineering at Purdue University. At the request of a few students, Dr. Yang began to teach Gongfu (Kung Fu), which resulted in the foundation of the Purdue University Chinese Kung Fu Research Club in the spring of 1975. While at Purdue, Dr. Yang also taught college-credited courses in Taijiquan. In May of 1978 he was awarded a Ph.D. in Mechanical Engineering by Purdue.

In 1980, Dr. Yang moved to Houston to work for Texas Instruments. While in Houston he founded Yang's Shaolin Kung Fu Academy, which was taken over by his student Mr. Jeffery Bolt after Dr. Yang moved to Boston in 1982. Dr. Yang founded Yang's Martial Arts Academy (YMAA) in Boston on October 1, 1982.

In January of 1984 Dr. Yang gave up his engineering career to devote more time to research, writing, and teaching. In March of 1986 he purchased property in the Jamaica Plain area of Boston to be used as the headquarters of the new organization, Yang's Martial Arts Association. The organization has continued to expand, and as of July 1st, 1989, YMAA has become just one division of Yang's Oriental Arts Association, Inc. (YOAA Inc.).

In summary, Dr. Yang has been involved in Chinese Wushu since 1961. During this time he has spent thirteen years learning Shaolin White Crane (Bai He), Shaolin Long Fist (Changquan), and Taijiquan. Dr. Yang has more than twenty years of instructional experience, and is regularly invited to offer seminars across the United States and around the world to share his knowledge of Chinese martial arts and Qigong.

Currently, YMAA has schools in the United States, Canada, Portugal, France, Italy, Poland, Holland, Hungary, Latvia, Saudi Arabia, and South Africa.

Dr. Yang, Jwing-Ming

FOREWORD
John P. Painter, Ph.D.

In the small town where I grew up in East Texas during the late 1940's and early 50's people slept with the windows open and the back door unlocked. Burglary, assault, murder, rape, and drug related crimes were things one read about in cheap detective novels, not in the local newspaper.

The same town in 1991 saw a shoot-out inside the halls of the local high school, gang members terrorizing citizens, and rape and murders have now become a monthly occurrence. Things have changed! Now everyone in almost every city in America lives behind locked doors and barred windows.

As a professional tactical trainer for many of our nation's police officers I know how bad things have become just in the past ten years. You should know that the police cannot always protect you from violent crime. In many cases they arrive after the assault, fill out a form, console the victim, and hope to catch the criminal. This does nothing to prevent the attack, heal the broken bones, or perhaps bury the dead. In the world of chaos and violence man has created for himself, training in a system of self-protection should no longer be looked upon as just a leisure time activity, hobby, or sport. It is the responsibility of each and every person young and old to learn some practical methods of crime prevention and defense. It should be our obligation to become skilled at sensing and dealing with danger in an appropriate manner in order to survive and to protect the safety of our children and loved ones.

I first met Dr. Yang, Jwing-Ming in 1987 at the United States National Chinese Martial Arts Competitions in Houston, Texas. Having read his books *Shaolin Chin Na, Shaolin Long Fist,* and *Yang Style Tai Chi Chuan,* I knew he possessed a great deal of knowledge about Chinese martial arts. Having used martial arts on the street for real, I am skeptical of many of today's "famous masters"; there are many who write and talk but who cannot truly do. After meeting Dr. Yang in person and observing his skill, I came away impressed that he is indeed one who can do as well as write.

I like to think that over the years we have become close friends, often sharing a room while presenting seminars at the Tai Chi Farm. I have learned to respect him as a sincere man who truly cares about the health and safety of all people. He has high moral standards and is possessed of the rare qualities of sincerity, compassion, and humility that should be, but so seldom are, the hallmarks of all true martial arts experts.

After carefully reading this manuscript, I believe the techniques presented here can be most useful to anyone who will take time to study, practice, and research them. Not only does Dr. Yang teach you how to use Chinese Gongfu (Kung Fu) for defense, but also a philosophy of how to recognize danger, avoid, and prevent attacks. I recommend that you read this book, study it and practice the methods, because the knowledge you will gain may one day save your life. This is real martial art!

1992, Arlington Texas
Captain John P. Painter, Ph.D.
Publisher, IAM Magazine
American Rangers Law Enforcement
Martial Training Institute

PREFACE
Yang, Jwing-Ming, Ph.D.

If we trace the history of Chinese martial arts in Western society, we can see that even before the 1960's, Karate and Judo had already been popular in the U.S. for nearly twenty years. Most Chinese culture was still hidden in communist China. Later, when Bruce Lee's motion pictures were introduced to the public, they presented a general concept of Chinese Gongfu (Kung Fu), which stimulated and excited Western oriental martial arts societies a great deal. Chinese Gongfu has since become popularly known in Western society.

At that time the term "Gongfu" was widely misinterpreted to mean "fighting," and very few people actually knew that the meaning of Gongfu is "hard work"; an endeavor which normally requires a great deal of time and energy to accomplish. It was even more amazing that, after the young generation saw these movies, they started to mix the concepts from what they had learned from movies with the background they had learned from Karate, Judo, Aikido, and their own imagination. This was the origin of American Style Chinese Gongfu, and hundreds of new Gongfu styles have been created. These practitioners did not know that the movies they had watched were a modified version of Chinese martial arts derived from Bruce Lee's training in Wing Chun (Yongchun) style. For cinematic purposes, they had been mixed with the concepts of Karate, Western Boxing, and some kicking techniques developed by Bruce Lee himself. At that time, there were only a very few traditional Chinese martial arts instructors residing in the West, and even fewer were teaching.

During this period Cheng, Man-Ching brought the concept of one Chinese internal martial art, Taijiquan, to the West. Through his teaching and publications, a limited portion of the public finally grasped the correct concepts of a small branch of Chinese martial arts.

This again brought to Western society a new paradigm for pursuing Chinese martial arts as they were traditionally trained. Taijiquan gradually became popular. However, American Style Chinese Gongfu still occupied the major market of the Chinese martial arts society in America.

When President Nixon levered open the tightly closed gate to mainland China in 1973, the Western public finally had a better chance to understand Chinese culture. From the more frequent communications, acupuncture techniques for medical purposes, used in China for more than four thousand years, were exported to the U. S. In addition, Chinese martial arts also slowly migrated westward. The period from the 1970's to the early 1980's can be regarded as an educational time for this cultural exchange. While the Americans' highly developed material sciences entered China, Chinese traditional medical and spiritual sciences (Qigong) started to influence American society.

But even with this increased exchange, today very few people understand the real meaning of Chinese martial arts training. Chinese Gongfu has a deep spiritual dimension that balances the physical training. That is why most of the Chinese martial arts were developed in Buddhist and Daoist monasteries. To many Chinese martial arts practitioners, training martial arts is only a way of understanding themselves and also the meaning of life.

In order to reach a high level of martial skill, you must continuously be humble, patient, ponder, and challenge yourself. During this process of learning and studying, the meaning of life can be deeply comprehended.

I have spent more than thirty-four years studying Chinese martial arts. But what is thirty-four years compared to the vast, profound, knowledge developed over more than five thousand years? My master told me: "The more bamboo grows, the lower it bows. What you are learning in martial arts are not the techniques of fighting but a way of your life." I did not understand it when I was twenty. Now that I am nearly fifty, I am starting to comprehend the deep meaning of these two sentences.

Since I resigned my engineering profession in 1984, I have put all my effort into teaching, writing, and publishing Chinese martial arts and Qigong, and I have never felt happier. It seems after so many years of scholarly study for my Ph.D., I finally discovered that my real happiness is introducing Chinese culture to the West. I have traveled to more than fifteen countries, and each year I spend more than two months in Europe, a few weeks in Saudi Arabia, and more than twenty weekends in different states across America. From this great demand, I can see that there are others who want to share in what I know.

However, it is not easy to convince younger generations that Chinese martial arts are for self cultivation and discipline, and not for fighting or glory. It is for internal understanding more than the external manifestation of dignity or pride. After much thought, I wrote this brief book of self-defense to capture the reader's interest in the arts. From here, I hope they will continue to search and study until they discover the meaning of their life.

Due to this reason, other than introducing practical psychological preparation and defense techniques for emergency situations, I have included a section on marital morality and many related stories. I hope through this effort, younger generations can be directed to the correct path of Chinese martial arts study.

INTRODUCTION

I was born in Taiwan one year after the end of World War II. Because of the ravages of the war, most people had to struggle to survive. In the next few years, as the democratic Goumindang party fought a civil war with the Communists, conditions grew even worse. For fifteen years the situation in Taiwan was difficult and unstable. This is the period in which I grew up. President Chiang Kai-Shek was planning a counterattack against the Communists to regain control of the mainland, but he also had to consider the survival and education of the people in Taiwan. Life was generally very hard, and it was especially so in families such as mine with nine children.

I remember I used to hate the world because of my physical and psychological suffering. I hated beauty, I disliked the rich, I cursed the whole of society, and I even despised myself. The only thing that could satisfy me was finding something exciting and challenging. I was a very troubled boy.

When I was fifteen, a classmate introduced me to White Crane Gongfu (Kung Fu), and I started studying with Master Cheng, Gin-Gsao. Master Cheng lived with his family in the mountains near my hometown of Xinzhu. It normally took me forty minutes to run from my home to where Master Cheng lived. I looked on this daily run and the training as a challenge. Day after day, month after month, I started to realize that what I was learning was not only the Crane fighting techniques, but also my master's way of life. I gradually became patient and persevering, and my willpower increased. Most important of all, however, I learned how to conquer myself. I learned how to control my emotional mind with my wisdom mind. I learned to clearly see what was right and what was wrong. After three years of training with Master Cheng, I was no longer a troublesome boy. Since then, Gongfu training has become the way through which I continue to learn more about life.

I always believed that I could use my personal experiences and knowledge to help promote the growth of a more stable society, so once I obtained my Ph.D. from Purdue University, I gradually started to pursue my dream. I hope that through publications, instruction, and seminars I can help others to better understand life.

This book is designed as an introduction to the martial arts for those people who are willing to accept the physical and mental challenges. However, people who would like to learn some simple techniques to defend themselves will also profit from this book. I believe that, while we should help other people and try to understand their problems, we should also learn how to defend ourselves from those who would make us their victims.

In Chapter 1 we will first discuss martial morality, and follow this with a historical survey of White Crane and Long Fist styles and a discussion of their foundations. In Chapter 2 we will analyze the psychology and strategies of self-defense. Chapter 3 will introduce some simple but effective defense techniques against barehand attacks, while Chapter 4 will present defense techniques against knife attacks.

CONTENTS

Chapter 1
Foundations

1-1. Martial Morality

Martial morality has always been one of the required disciplines in Chinese martial society. Before you learn martial techniques, you should first understand this subject.

In Chinese martial society, it is well known that the success of a student is not determined by his external appearance, or by how strong or weak he is, but rather by the student's way of thinking and his or her morality. Chinese martial artists have a saying: "A student will spend three years looking for a good teacher, and a teacher will test a student for three years." A wise student realizes that it is better to spend several years looking for a good teacher than to spend the time learning from a mediocre one. A good teacher will lead you to the right path, and help you to build a strong foundation for your future training. A teacher who is not qualified, however, will not help you build a strong foundation, and may even teach you many bad habits. In addition, good teachers will always set a good example for their students with their spiritual and moral virtue. Good martial arts teachers do not teach only martial techniques, they also teach a way of life.

From the point of view of a teacher, it is very hard to find good students. When people have just begun their studies, they are usually enthusiastic and sincere, and they are willing to accept discipline and observe proper manners. However, as time passes, you gradually get to see what they are really like, and sometimes it's quite different from how they acted in the beginning. Because of this, teachers quite frequently spend at least three years watching and testing students before they decide whether they can trust them and pass on to them the secrets of their style. This was especially so in ancient times when martial arts were used in wars, and fighting techniques were kept secret.

Martial Morality is called "Wude." Teachers have long considered Wude to be the most important criterion for judging students, and they have made it the most important part of the training in the traditional Chinese martial arts. Wude includes two aspects: the morality of deed and the morality of mind. Morality of deed includes: **HUMILITY, RESPECT, RIGHTEOUSNESS, TRUST, AND LOYALTY**. Morality of mind consists of: **WILL, ENDURANCE, PERSEVERANCE, PATIENCE, AND COURAGE**. Traditionally, only those students who had cultivated these standards of morality were considered to be worthy of teaching. Of the two aspects of morality, the morality of deed is more important. The reason for this is very simple. Morality of deed concerns the student's relationship with master and classmates, other martial artists, and the general public. Students who are not moral in their actions are not worthy of being taught, since they cannot be trusted or even respected. Furthermore, without morality of deed, they may abuse the art and use their fighting ability to harm innocent people. Therefore, masters will normally watch their students carefully for a long time until they are sure that the students have matched their standards of morality of deed before letting them start serious training.

Morality of mind is for the self-cultivation which is required for reaching the final goal. The Chinese consider that we have two minds, an "emotional mind" (Xin) and a "wisdom mind" (Yi). Usually, when a person fails in something it is because the emotional mind has dominated the thinking. The five elements in the morality of mind are the keys to training, and they lead the student to the stage where the wisdom mind can dominate. This self-cultivation and discipline should be the goal of any martial arts training philosophy.

Next, we will discuss these requirements of morality.

Martial Morality
(Wude, 武德)

Morality of Deed:
1. **Humility (Qian Xu; 謙虛)**

Humility comes from controlling your feelings of pride. In China it is said: "Satisfaction (i.e., pride) loses, humility earns benefits."(*1) When you are satisfied with yourself, you will not think deeply, and you will not be willing to learn. However, if you remain humble, you will always be looking for ways to better yourself, and you will keep on learning. Remember, there is no limitation to knowledge. It does not matter how deep you have reached, there is always a deeper level. Confucius said, "If three people walk by, there must be one of them who can be my teacher."(*2) There is always someone who is more talented or more knowledgeable than you in some field. The Chinese say: "There is always a man beyond the man, there is a sky above the sky."(*3) Since this is so, how can you be proud of yourself?

I remember a story that my White Crane master told me when I was seventeen years old. Once there was a bamboo that had just popped up out of the ground. It looked at the sky and smiled, and said to itself, "Someone told me that the sky is so high that it cannot be reached. I don't believe that's true." The sprout was young and felt strong. It believed that if it kept growing, one day it could reach the sky. So it kept growing and growing. Ten years passed, twenty years passed. Again it looked at the sky. The sky was still very high, and it was still far beyond its reach. Finally, it realized something, and started to bow down. The more it grew the lower it bowed. My teacher asked me to always remember that "The taller the bamboo grows, the lower it bows."(*4)

There was another story a friend told me. Once upon a time, a student came to see a Zen master. He said, "Honorable Master, I have studied for many years, and I have learned so much of the martial arts and Zen theory already that I have reached a very high level. I heard that you are a great master, and I have therefore come to see if you can teach me anything more."

The master didn't reply. Instead, he picked up a teacup and placed it in front of the student. He then picked up the teapot and poured until the tea reached the rim of the cup, and then he kept on pouring until the tea overflowed onto the table. The student stared at the master in total confusion and said, "No, No, Master! The cup is overflowing!"

The master stopped pouring, looked at him and smiled. He said, "Young man, this is you. I am sorry that I cannot accept you as a student. Like this cup, your mind is filled up and I cannot teach you any more. If you want to learn, you must first empty your cup."

In order to be humble, you must first get rid of your false dignity. This is especially true in front of a master. A person who is really wise knows when and how to bend, and always keeps his cup empty.

2. Respect (Zun Jing; 尊敬)

Respect is the foundation of your relationship with your parents, teachers, your fellow students, other martial artists, and all other people in this society. Respect makes a harmonious relationship possible. However, the most important type of respect is self-respect. If you can't respect yourself, how can you respect others or expect them to respect you? Respect must be earned, you cannot ask for it or demand it.

In China, it is said: "Those who respect themselves and others will also be respected."(*5) For example, if you despise yourself and become a villain in this society, then you have lost your self-respect. Since you have abused your personality and humility as a human, why should other people respect you? Only when you have demonstrated that you are deserving of respect will respect come to you automatically and naturally.

I remember my grandmother told me a story. A long time ago a girl named Li-Li got married, and went to live with her husband and mother-in-law. In a very short time Li-Li found that she couldn't get along with her mother-in-law at all. Their personalities were very different, and Li-Li was infuriated by many of her mother-in-law's habits. In addition, she criticized Li-Li constantly.

Days passed days, weeks passed weeks, and Li-Li and her mother-in-law never stopped arguing and fighting. But what made the situation even worse was that, according to ancient Chinese tradition, Li-Li had to bow to her mother-in-law and obey her every wish. All the anger and unhappiness in the house was causing the poor husband great distress.

Finally, Li-Li could not stand her mother-in-law's bad temper and dictatorship any longer, so she decided to do something about it. Li-Li went to see her father's good friend Mr. Huang, who sold herbs. She told him the problem, and asked if he would give her some poison so that she could solve the problem once and for all.

Mr. Huang thought for a while, and finally he said, "Li-Li, I will help you to solve your problem, but you must listen to me and obey what I tell you." Li-Li said, "Yes, Mr. Huang, I will do whatever you tell me to do." Mr. Huang went into the back room, and returned in a few minutes with a package of herbs. He told Li-Li, "You can't use a quick-acting poison to get rid of your mother-in-law, because that would cause people to become suspicious. Therefore, I have given you a number of herbs that will slowly build up poison in her body. Every other day prepare some pork or chicken, and put a little of these herbs in her serving. Now, in order to make sure that nobody suspects you when she dies, you must be very careful to act very friendly toward her. Don't argue with her, obey her every wish, and treat her like a queen."

Li-Li was so happy. She thanked Mr. Huang, and hurried home to start her plot of murdering her mother-in-law. Weeks went by, and months went by, and every other day Li-Li served the specially treated food to her mother-in-law. She remembered what Mr. Huang had said about avoiding suspicion, so she controlled her temper, obeyed her mother-in-law, and treated her like her own mother.

After six months had passed, the whole household had changed. Li-Li had practiced controlling her temper so much that she found that she almost never got mad or upset. She hadn't had an argument in six months with her mother-in-law, who now seemed much kinder and easier to get along with. The mother-in-law's attitude toward Li-Li had changed, and she began to love Li-Li like her own daughter. She kept telling friends and relatives that Li-Li was the best daughter-in-law one could ever find. Li-Li and her mother-in-law were now treating each other just like a real mother and daughter. Li-Li's husband was very happy to see what was happening.

One day Li-Li came to see Mr. Huang and asked for his help again. She said, "Dear Mr. Huang, please help me to keep the poison from killing my mother-in-law! She's changed into such a nice women, and I love her like my own mother. I do not want her to die because of the poison I gave to her."

Mr. Huang smiled and nodded his head. "Li-Li," he said, "there's nothing to worry about. I never gave you any poison. All of the herbs I gave you were simply to improve her health. The only poison was in your mind and your attitude toward her, but that has been all washed away by the love which you gave to her."

From this story you can see that before anyone can respect you, you must first respect others. Remember, "The person who loves others will also be loved."

There was also another story my grandmother told me. In China, there was once a family made up of a father, a mother, a ten year old son, and a grandmother. Every mealtime they sat together around the table. The grandmother was quite old. Her hands had begun to shake all the time, and she had difficulty holding things. Whenever she ate, she couldn't hold the rice bowl steady and spilled rice all over the table.

The daughter-in-law was very upset by this. One day she complained to her husband, "My dear husband, every time your mother eats she spills her food all over the table. This makes me so sick I can't eat my own food!" The husband didn't say anything. He knew that he couldn't keep his mother's hands from shaking.

In a few days, when the husband had not done anything to solve the problem, his wife spoke to him again. "Are you going to do something about your mother or not? I cannot stand it any more." After arguing for a while, the husband sadly gave in to his wife's suggestion, and agreed that his mother should sit at a separate table, away from the rest of the family. When dinnertime came, the grandmother found herself sitting alone at a separate table. And to make things worse, she had to eat from a cheap, chipped bowl because she had dropped and broken several others.

The grandmother was very sad, but she knew she couldn't do anything about it. She began to think of the past, and how much time and love she had given her son as he was growing up. She had never complained, but had always been there when he was sick or when he needed anything. Now she felt deserted by her family, and her heart was broken.

Several days passed. The grandmother was still very sad, and the smile began to disappear from her face. Her ten year old grandson had been watching everything, and he came to her and said, "Grandma, I know you are very unhappy about how my parents are treating you, but don't worry. I think I know how to get them to invite you back to the table, but I'll need your help."

Hope began to grow in the grandmother's heart. "But what do you want me to do?" she asked. The boy smiled and said, "Tonight at dinnertime, break your rice bowl, but make it look like an accident." Grandmother's eyes opened wide in wonder. "But why?" she asked. "Don't worry," he said, "leave it to me."

Dinnertime came. She was curious about what her grandson was going to do, so she decided to do as he had asked. When her son and daughter-in-law were not looking, she picked up the old and chipped rice bowl that she had to eat out of, and dropped it on the floor and broke it. Immediately her daughter-in-law stood up, ready to complain. However, before she could say anything, the grandson stood up and said, "Grandma, why did you break that bowl? I was going to save it for my mother when she gets old!"

When the mother heard this her face turned pale. She suddenly realized that everything she did was an example for her son. The way she was treating her mother-in-law was teaching her son how to treat her when she got old. She suddenly felt very ashamed. From that day on, the whole family ate together around the same table.

From this, you can see that how we love and respect teachers and elders is exactly how we deserve to be treated when we are old. Real love is something that cannot be purchased. Respect your parents and love them always. Only then will you deserve the respect and love of your own children.

3. Righteousness (Zheng Yi; 正義)

Righteousness is a way of life. Righteousness means that if there is something you should do, you don't hesitate to take care of it, and if there is something that you should not do, you don't get involved with it. Your wisdom mind should be the leader, not your emotional mind. If you can do this, then you will feel clear spiritually, and avoid being plagued by feelings of guilt. If you can demonstrate this kind of personality, you will be able to avoid evil influences, and you will earn the trust of others.

In the period of the Warring States (475-222 B.C.), the two neighboring states of Zhao and Qin were often fighting against each other. There were two capable and talented officers in Zhao's court, a military commander named Lian Bo and a civilian official named Lin Xiang-Ru. Because of these two men, the state of Qin dared not launch a full-scale invasion against Zhao.

Originally, Lin Xiang-Ru's position was far lower than that of General Lian Bo. But later on, when Lin Xiang-Ru was assigned as an ambassador to Qin, he won a diplomatic victory for the Zhao. Because of this, the Zhao king began to assign him to more important positions, and before too long his rank was higher than Lian Bo's. Lian Bo was very unhappy, and unwilling to accept this. He kept telling his subordinates that he would find an opportunity to humiliate Lin Xiang-Ru.

When Lin Xiang-Ru heard of this, he avoided meeting Lian Bo face to face at every occasion. One day, some of Lin Xiang-Ru's officers came to see him and said to him, "General Lian Bo has only talked about what he intends to do, yet you have already become so afraid. We feel very humiliated and would like to resign."

Lin Xiang-Ru then asked them, "If you were to compare General Lian Bo and the Qin's King, who would be more prestigious?" "Of course General Lian Bo cannot compare with the King of Qin!" they replied.

"Right!" he exclaimed. "And when I was an ambassador to Qin I had the courage to denounce the King of Qin right to his face. Thus, I have no fear of General Lian Bo! The State of Qin dares not attack Zhao because of General Lian Bo and myself. If the two of us are at odds with each other, Qin will take advantage of this opportunity to invade us. The interests of the country come first with me, and I am not going to haggle with Lian Bo because of personal hostilities!"

Later, when Lian Bo heard of this, he felt extremely ashamed. He tore off his shirt, and with a birch rod tied to his back, he went to Lin Xiang-Ru's home to request retribution for his own false dignity. Lin Xiang-Ru modestly helped Lian Bo up from the ground and held his hand firmly. From that time on, Lian Bo and Lin Xiang-Ru became close friends and served their country with the same heart.

There was another story that happened during the Chinese Spring and Autumn Period (722-481 B.C.). In the state of Jin, there was a high-ranking official named Qi Xi. When he was old and ready to retire, Duke Dao of Jin asked him to recommend a candidate to replace himself. Qi Xi said, "Xie Hu is an excellent man who is most suitable to replace me."

Duke Dao was very curious and said, "Isn't Xie Hu your political enemy? Why do you recommend him?" "You asked me who I thought was most suitable and most trustworthy for the job. Therefore, I recommended who I thought was best for this position. You did not ask me who was my enemy," Qi Xi replied.

Unfortunately, before Duke Dao could assign Xie Hu the new position, Xie Hu died. Duke Dao could only ask Qi Xi to recommend another person for his position. Qi Xi said, "Now that Xie Hu is dead, the only person who can take my place is Qi Wu."

Duke Dao was again very curious and said, "Isn't Qi Wu your son? Aren't you afraid that there may be gossip?" "You asked me only who was the most suitable for the position and did not asked if Qi Wu was my son. I only replied with who was the best choice as a replacement."

As Qi Xi predicted, his son Qi Wu was able to contribute greatly. People believed that only a virtuous man like Qi Xi could recommend a really talented man. He would not praise an enemy to flatter him, and he would not promote his own son out of selfishness.

4. Trust (Xin Yong; 信用)

Trust includes being trustworthy, and also trusting yourself. You must develop a personality which other people can trust. For example, you should not make promises lightly, but if you have made a promise, you should fulfill it. Trust is the key to friendship and the best way of earning respect. The trust of a friend is hard to gain, but easy to lose. Self-trust is the root of confidence. You must learn to build up your confidence and demonstrate it externally. Only then can you earn the trust and respect of others.

There is an ancient Chinese story about Emperor You of Zhou (781-771 B.C.). When Emperor You attacked the kingdom of Bao, he won a beautiful lady named Bao Si. However, although she was beautiful, Bao Si never smiled. In order to make her smile, the Emperor gave her precious pearls and jewels to wear, and delicious things to eat. He tried a thousand things but still Bao Si wouldn't smile. The Emperor was the monarch of the country and yet he couldn't win a smile from the beautiful lady. It made him very unhappy.

At that time, the country of Zhou had platforms for signal fires around the borders. If an enemy attacked the capital, the fires were lit to signal the feudal lords that their emperor was in danger, and they would immediately send out their troops to help. The fires were not to be lit unless the situation was critical. However, the emperor thought of a way to use them to please Bao Si. He ordered the signal fires lit. The feudal lords thought that the capital city was in great danger, so a vast and mighty army of soldiers soon came running.

When Bao Si saw all the troops rushing crazily about in a nervous frenzy, she unconsciously let out a great laugh. Emperor You was so extremely happy that he smiled and smiled, and completely forgot about the lords standing there staring blankly. After a while the Emperor said, "It's nothing. Everyone go home."

Emperor You completely forgot about the importance of the signal fires, and went so far as to light them several times in order to win Bao Si's smile. The lords all knew that they had been made fools of, and were furious.

Later, Emperor You dismissed his empress, Lady Shen, in favor of his concubine Bao Si. Lady Shen's father was greatly angered and united with a foreign tribe called the Quan Rong to attack Emperor You. When Emperor You's situation got urgent, he ordered the signal fires to be lit to summon the feudal lords to save him and the capital. Even as he was being killed, the Emperor could not understand that because of the games he had been playing with the signal fires, not even one lord would come to save him.

5. Loyalty (Zhong Cheng; 忠誠)

Loyalty is the root of trust. You should be loyal to your teacher and to your friends, and they should also be loyal to you. Loyalty lets mutual trust grow. In the Chinese martial arts, it is especially crucial that there be loyalty between you and your master. This loyalty is built upon a foundation of obedience to your master. Obedience is the prerequisite for learning. If you sincerely desire to learn, you should get rid of your dignity. You must bow to your teacher both mentally and spiritually. Only this will open the gates of trust. A teacher will not teach someone who is always concerned about his own dignity. Remember, in front of your teacher, you do not have dignity.

There was a story told to me when I was a child. A long time ago in Asia there was a king. Nobody had ever seen the king's real face, because whenever he met with his ministers and officials, and whenever he appeared in public, he always wore a mask. The face on the mask had a very stern and solemn expression. Because nobody could see the real expression on his face, all the officials and people respected him, obeyed him, and feared him. This made it possible for him to rule the country efficiently and well.

One day his wife said to him, "If you have to wear the mask in order to rule the country well, then what the people respect and show loyalty to is the mask and not you." The king wanted to prove to his wife that it was he who really ruled the country, and not the mask, so he decided to take the mask off and let the officials see his real face.

Without the mask, the officials were able to see the expression on his face and figure out what he was thinking. It wasn't long before the officials weren't afraid of him anymore.

A few months passed, and the situation got steadily worse. He had lost the solemn dignity which made people fear him, and even worse, the officials had started to lose respect for him. Not only did they argue with each other in front of him, they even began to argue with him about his decisions.

He soon realized that the unity and cooperation among his officials had disintegrated. His ability to lead the country had gradually disappeared, and the country was falling into disorder. The king realized that, in order to regain the respect of the people and his ability to rule the country, he had to do something. He therefore gave the order to behead all of the officials who had seen his face, and he then appointed new ones. He then put the mask back on his face. Soon afterward, the country was again united and under his control.

Do you have a mask on your face? Is it the mask that people are loyal to? Is what you show people on your face what you really think? Do we have to put a mask on in this masked society? How heavy and how thick is your mask? Have you ever taken your mask off and taken a good look at the real you in the mirror? If you can do this it will make you humble. Then, even if you have a mask on your face, your life will not be ruled by your mask.

Morality of Mind:
1. Will (Yi Zhi; 意志)
It usually takes a while to demonstrate a strong will. This is because of the struggle between the emotional mind and the wisdom mind. If your wisdom mind governs your entire being, you will be able to suppress the disturbances that come from the emotional mind, and your will can last. A strong will depends upon the sincerity with which you commit yourself to your goal. This has to come from deep within you, and can't be just a casual, vague desire. Oftentimes, the students who show the greatest eagerness to learn in the beginning, quit the soonest, while those who hide their eagerness deep inside their hearts stay the longest.

There is a Chinese story from ancient times about a ninety year old man who lived together with his sons, daughters-in-law, and grandsons near the mountain Bei. In front of his house were two mountains, Taixing and Wangwu, which blocked the road to the county seat and made travel very inconvenient. One day he decided to remove these two mountains to the coast nearby and dump the dirt into the sea. His neighbors laughed at him when they heard of this. However, he replied, "Why is this so impossible? I will die soon, but I have sons and my sons will have grandsons without end. However, the mountain remains the same. Why can't I move it?" Isn't it true that where there is a will, there is success?

There is another story about the famous poet Li Bai. When Li Bai was young he studied at a school far away from his home. He lacked a strong will, so before the end of his studies he gave up and decided to go home. While crossing over a mountain on the way home he passed an old lady sitting in front of her house. In her hands she held a metal pestle which she was grinding on the top of a rock. Li Bai was very curious and asked her what she was doing. She said, "I want to grind this pestle into a needle." When Li Bai heard of this he was very ashamed, and decided to return to school and finish his studies. He later became one of the greatest poets in China.

There is another well-known story which tells of a famous archer named Hou Yi. When Hou Yi heard that there was a famous archery master in the North, he decided to ask the master to take him as a student. After three months of travel, Hou Yi finally arrived in the cold Northern territory. Before long, he found the home of the famous master. He knocked on the door, and when the old master came out, Hou Yi knelt down and said, "Honorable master, would you please accept me as your disciple?" The old master replied, "Young man, I can't accept any students. I am not as good as you think, and besides, I am already old." But Hou Yi would not accept no for an answer. "Honorable master," he said, "I have made up my mind: I swear I will not get up until you promise to take me as your student."

The master closed the door without a word, leaving Hou Yi outside. Before long it got dark and started to snow, but Hou Yi remained in his kneeling position without moving. One whole day passed, but the master never appeared again. Hou Yi continued to kneel on the ground in front of the door. A second day passed, and a third day. Finally, the master opened the door and said, "Young man, if you really want to learn my archery techniques, you must first pass a few tests." "Of course, master," Hou Yi replied with great happiness.

"The first is a test of your patience and perseverance. You must go back home and every morning and evening watch three sticks of incense burn out. Do this for three years and then come back to see me."

Hou Yi went home and started to watch the incense each morning and evening. At first, he got bored and impatient very quickly. However, he was determined to keep his promise, so he continued to watch the incense. Six months later, watching the incense burn had become a habit. He started to realize that he had become patient, and even began to enjoy his morning and evening routine. He began to concentrate his mind, focusing on the head of the incense as it burned down the stick. From practicing concentration and calming his mind, he learned to distinguish between the real and the false. After the three years were up, he found that every time he concentrated and focused his eyes on something, that object would be enlarged in his mind, and all other surrounding objects would disappear. He did not realize that he had learned the most important factor in becoming a good archer - a concentrated and calm mind. After he finished this test, he was very happy and traveled to the North to see his master.

The master told him, "You have passed the first test, now you must pass a second. You must go back and day and night watch your wife weave at her loom, following the shuttle with your eyes as it moves incessantly to and fro. You must do this for three years and then come back to see me."

Hou Yi was very disappointed, because he had thought that his master would teach him now that he had completed his three years of patience training. However, because his heart was set on learning from this famous master, he left and went home. He sat by his wife's loom and focused his eyes on the shuttle as it moved to and fro. As with the incense, he didn't enjoy himself at first, but after one year passed he began to get used to the fast shuttle motion. After another two years, he found that when he concentrated on the shuttle, it would move more slowly. Without realizing it, he had learned the next important part of an archer's training - concentrating on a moving object. He returned to his master and told his master what he had found. Instead of beginning his instruction, he was asked to return home and make 10 rice baskets a day for the next three years. Chinese rice baskets were made out of rattan, and one needed to have very strong wrists and arms to make them. Even a very good basket maker could hardly make five a day, and Hou Yi was being asked to make ten a day!

Although disappointed, Hou Yi returned home to do as he was told. In the beginning he hardly slept, spending almost every hour of the day in making baskets. His hands were numb and bleeding, his shoulders were sore, and he was always tired, but he persisted in working to finish ten baskets a day. After six months he found that his hands and shoulders were no longer in pain, and he could make ten baskets a day easily. By the end of three years, he could make twenty a day. He surely had achieved the last requirement of a good archer - strong and steady arms and shoulders. Hou Yi finally realized that all his efforts for the last nine years had actually been the training for how to become a good archer. He was now able to shoot very well with his concentrated mind and strong arms.

Proud and happy, he returned to his master, who said, "You have studied hard and learned well. I can't teach you any more than what you already know." With this the master turned his head and walked away.

Hou Yi was thinking that all his master had taught him in the last nine years was expressed in only three sentences. He couldn't believe that this was all there was to learn. He decided to put his master, who by now was two hundred yards away, to a test. He pulled an arrow from his quiver, aimed at the tassel on his master's hat, and released. His master instantly sensed the arrow coming his way, pulled and notched an arrow, and shot it back to meet the coming arrow in the air. Both arrows dropped to the ground. Hou Yi saw this and without stopping shot a second arrow, and this second arrow suffered the same fate. He couldn't believe that his master could shoot and meet his arrows in mid-air three times in a row, so he loosed a third arrow. He suddenly realized that his master had run out of arrows. While he was wondering what his master was going to do, his master plucked a branch from a nearby willow tree and used this branch as an arrow. Again it met Hou Yi's arrow in mid-air. This time, Hou Yi ran toward his master, knelt before him, and said, "Most respected master, now I realize one thing. The thing that I cannot learn from you is experience, which can only come from practicing by myself."

Of course, part of the story is exaggerated. However, masters in China often used this story to encourage the students to strengthen their will, to think, and to research. What the master can give you is a key to the door. To enter the door and find things inside is your own responsibility. The more experience you have, the better you will be.

2. Endurance, Perseverance, and Patience (Ren Nai, Yi Li, Heng Xin; 忍耐，毅力，恒心)

Endurance, perseverance, and patience are the manifestations of a strong will. People who are successful are not always the smartest ones, but they are always the ones who are patient and who persevere. People who are really wise do not use wisdom only to guide their thinking, they also use it to govern their personalities. Through cultivating these three elements you will gradually build up a profound mind, which is the key to the deepest essence of learning. If you know how to use your mind to ponder as you train, it can lead you to a deeper stage of understanding. If you can manifest this understanding in your actions, you will be able to surpass others.

Of all the stories that my master told me, my favorite one is about the boy who carved the Buddha. Once upon a time, there was a twelve year old boy whose parents had been killed during a war. He came to the Shaolin Temple and asked to see the Head Priest. When he was led to the Head Priest, the boy knelt down and said, "Honorable Master, would you please accept me as your Gongfu student? I will respect, obey, and serve you well, and I won't disappoint you."

As the Head Priest looked at the boy, he felt that he had to give him a test before he could accept him as a student. He said, "Boy, I would like to teach you Gongfu, but I have to leave the temple for one year to preach. Could you do me a favor while I am gone?" The boy was glad to have a chance to prove that he could be a good student, and so he said, "Certainly, honorable Master! What do you want me to do?"

The Head Priest led the boy out of the temple and pointed to a big tree. He said, "I have always wanted a good carving of the Buddha. See that tree? Could you chop it down and make a Buddha for me?" The boy replied enthusiastically, "Yes, Master! When you return, I will have finished the Buddha for you." The next morning the Head Priest departed, leaving the boy to live with the monks. A few days later the boy chopped down the tree, and got ready to make the Buddha. The boy wanted to carve a beautiful Buddha and make the Head Priest happy. He worked night and day, patiently carving as carefully as he could.

A year later the Head Priest came back from his preaching. The boy was very anxious and excited. He showed the Head Priest his Buddha, which was five feet tall. He hoped to earn the Head Priest's trust, and he eagerly waited to be praised. But the Head Priest looked at the Buddha, and he knew that the boy had sincerely done his best. However, he decided to give the boy a further test. He said, "Boy, it is well done. But it seems it is too big for me. It is not the size which I was expecting. Since I have to leave the temple again to preach for another year, could you use this time to make this Buddha smaller?"

The boy was very disappointed and unhappy. He had thought that when the Head Priest saw the Buddha, he would be accepted as a student and he could start his Gongfu training. However, in order to make the Head Priest happy he said, "Yes, Master. I will make it smaller." Even though the boy had agreed, the Head Priest could see from the boy's face that this time he did not agree willingly, from his heart. However, he knew that this time the test would be a real one.

Next morning the Head Priest left, and again the boy stayed with the monks to fulfill this promise. The boy started carving the Buddha, trying to make it smaller, but he was disappointed and very unhappy. However, he forced himself to work. After six months had gone by, he found that he had carved an ugly, unhappy Buddha.

The boy was very depressed. He found that he couldn't work on the Buddha when he was so unhappy, so he stopped working. Days passed days, weeks passed weeks. The date of the Head Priest's return was getting closer. His chances of becoming a student of the Head Priest were getting slimmer and slimmer, and his unhappiness was growing deeper and deeper.

One morning, he suddenly realized an important thing. He said to himself, "If completing the Buddha is the only way I can learn Gongfu, why don't I make it good and enjoy it?" After that, his attitude changed. Not only was he happy again, he also regained his patience and his will was stronger. Day and night he worked. The more he worked, the happier he was, and the more he enjoyed his work. Before the boy noticed it, the year was up and he had almost completed his happy and refined Buddha.

When the Head Priest came back, the boy came to see him with his new Buddha. This carving was two feet tall, and smiling. When the priest saw the Buddha, he was very pleased. He knew that the boy had accomplished one of the hardest challenges that a person can face: conquering himself. However, he decided to give the boy one final test. He said, "Boy, you have done well. But it seems it is still too big for me. In a few days I have to leave the temple again for another year of preaching. During this time, could you make this Buddha even smaller?" Surprisingly, this time the boy showed no sign of being disappointed. Instead, he said, "No problem, Master. I will make it smaller." The boy had learned how to enjoy his work.

The Head Priest left again. This time, the boy enjoyed his work. Every minute he could find he spent at his task, carefully making the carving more lifelike and refined. His sincerity, his patience, and his growing maturity became expressed in the Buddha's face.

One year later, the Head Priest returned. The boy handed him a Buddha which was only two inches tall, and which had the best artwork one could ever find. The Head Priest now believed that this boy would be a successful martial artist. The boy had passed the test. He went on to become one of the best students in the Shaolin Temple.

As mentioned earlier, we have two kinds of minds. One comes from our emotions, and the other is generated from our wisdom and clear judgment. Do you remember times when you knew you should do a certain thing, but at the same time you didn't want to do it? It was your wisdom mind telling you to do it, and your lazy emotional mind saying no. Which side won? Once you can follow what your wisdom mind tells you to do, you will have conquered yourself and you will surely be successful.

3. Courage (Yong Gan; 勇敢)

Courage is often confused with bravery. Courage originates with the understanding that comes from the wisdom mind. Bravery is the external manifestation of courage, and can be considered to be the child of the wisdom and the emotional minds. For example, if you have the courage to accept a challenge, that means your mind has understood the situation and made a decision. Next, you must be brave enough to face the challenge. Without courage, the bravery cannot last long. Without the profound comprehension of courage, bravery can be blind and stupid.

Daring to face a challenge that you think needs to be faced is courage. But successfully manifesting courage requires more than just a decision from your wisdom mind. You also need a certain amount of psychological preparation so that you can be emotionally balanced; this will give your bravery a firm root so that it can endure. Frequently you do not have enough time to think and make a decision. A wise person always prepares, considering the possible situations that might arise, so that when something happens he will be ready and can demonstrate bravery.

There is a story from China's Spring and Autumn period (722-481 B.C.). At that time, there were many feudal lords who each controlled a part of the land, and who frequently attacked one another.

When an army from the nation of Jin attacked the nation of Zheng, the Zheng ruler sent a delegation to the Jin army to discuss conditions for their withdrawal. Duke Wen of Jin (636-627 B.C.) made two demands: first, that the young duke Lan be set up as heir apparent; second, that the high official Shu Zhan, who opposed Lan's being made heir apparent, be handed over to the Jin. The Zheng ruler refused to assent to the second condition.

Shu Zhan said, "Jin has specified that it wants me. If I do not go, the Jin armies that now surround us will certainly not withdraw. Wouldn't I then be showing myself to be afraid of death and insufficiently loyal?" "If you go," said the Zheng ruler, "you will certainly die. Thus I cannot bear to let you go."

"What is so bad about letting a minister go to save the people and secure the nation?" asked Shu Zhan. The ruler of Zheng then, with tears in his eyes, sent some men to escort Shu Zhan to the Jin encampment.

When Duke Wen of Jin saw Shu Zhan, he was furious and immediately ordered that a large tripod be prepared to cook him to death. Shu Zhan, however, was not the least bit afraid. "I hope that I can finish speaking before you kill me," he said. Duke Wen told him to speak quickly.

Relaxed, Shu Zhan said, "Before, while you were in Zheng, I often praised your virtue and wisdom in front of others, and I thought that after you returned to Jin you would definitely become the most powerful among the feudal lords. After the alliance negotiations at Wen, I also advised my lord to follow Jin. Unfortunately, he did not accept my suggestion. Now you think that I am guilty, but my lord knows that I am innocent and stubbornly refused to deliver me to you. I was the one who asked to come and save Zheng from danger. I am this kind of person, accurately forecasting events is called wisdom, loving one's country with all one's heart is called loyalty, not fleeing in the face of danger is called courage, and being willing to die to save one's country is called benevolence. I find it hard to believe that a benevolent, wise, loyal, and courageous minister can be killed in Jin!" Then, leaning against the tripod, he cried, "From now on, those who would serve their rulers should remember what happens to me!"

Duke Wen's expression changed greatly after hearing this speech. He ordered that Shu Zhan be spared and had him escorted back to Zheng.

There is another story about a famous minister, Si Ma-Guang, and his childhood during the Song dynasty (1019-1086 A.D.). When he was a child, he was playing with a few of his playmates in a garden where there was a giant cistern full of water next to a tree.

One of the children was very curious about what was in the giant cistern. Since the cistern was much taller than the child, he climbed up the tree to see inside. Unfortunately, he slipped and fell into the cistern and started to drown.

When this happened, all of the children were so scared and they did not know what to do. Some of them were so afraid that they immediately ran away. Si Ma-Guang, however, without hesitation picked up a big rock and threw it at the cistern and broke it. The water inside flowed out immediately, and the child inside was saved.

This story teaches that when a crisis occurs, in addition to wisdom and a calm mind, you must also be brave enough to execute your decision.

1-2. History of the White Crane and Long Fist Martial Styles

In China, most martial art styles have never kept formal, official records. Instead, the history of each style was passed down orally from generation to generation. After being passed down for many years, with new stories being added occasionally, the history eventually turned into a story. In many instances, a more accurate record can actually be obtained from martial novels written at that time, since they were based on the customs and actual events of the time. For example, the novels "Historical Drama of Shaolin" (Shaolin Yan Yi) by Shao Yu-Sheng, and "Qian Long Visits South of the River" (Qian Long Xia Jiang Nan) by an unknown author, were written during the Qing dynasty about two hundred years ago.(*6,*7) In these novels, the characters and background are all based on real people and events of the time. Of course, some liberties were taken with the truth, but since the novels were meant to be read by the public at that time, they had to be based very strongly on fact. Because of these and other similar novels, most martial styles are able to trace back their histories with some degree of accuracy.

This is the case with the history of the White Crane style. You may therefore treat the following historical survey as a story or as an informal history. Actually, no one can be sure how accurate it is. The history described here is based on the oral transmission from my White Crane Master and also on a number of novels (mainly "Historical Drama of Shaolin").

It is known that the Shaolin temple was built in 377 A.D. on Shaoshi Mountain, Deng Feng Xian, Henan province, on the order of Emperor Wei. The emperor built the temple for a Buddhist named Ba Tuo (Happy Buddha) for the purpose of preaching and worship. It is known that at this time the monks did not do any martial training. In 527 A.D. during the Liang dynasty a Buddhist named Da Mo, who was a prince of an Indian tribe, was invited to China by Emperor Liang to preach Buddhism. When the Emperor did not like Da Mo's Buddhist philosophy, Da Mo retired to the Shaolin temple. While there he wrote two Qigong classics: "Yi Jin Jing" and "Xi Sui Jing." Da Mo died in 539 A.D.

After Da Mo, the Shaolin monks used the Yi Jin Jing and Xi Sui Jing training to strengthen their physical bodies, and also their spiritual bodies for Buddhahood. Gradually, martial techniques were created at Shaolin to help the monks defend the property of the temple from bandits. It is known that the martial arts training at that time included the fighting techniques of the five animal patterns. They are Crane, Snake, Dragon, Leopard, and Tiger. This means that the Crane style actually originated around the 6th century.

It is said that later, in the beginning of the Qing dynasty (1644 A.D.), a monk named "Xinglong," who specialized in the Crane style, was sent by the Shaolin temple to Tibet to study Tibetan Buddhism. Before he died there he passed down the Crane style, which became known as "La Ma," or the "Northern White Crane" system.

Later, the Crane style was passed down to Canton, Fujian, Taiwan, and Indochina. After nearly three hundred years of modification, what has become known as the Southern Crane Style gradually emerged. It specializes in using the hands for short range fighting.

Today, there are four known southern Crane styles: Sleeping Crane or Trembling Crane (Su He, Zong He, or Zhan He), Shouting Crane (Ming He), Eating Crane (Shi He), and Flying Crane (Fei He). Many of these styles use the basic sequence "San Zhan" for their basic training. Internally, all of the styles discuss how to sink the Qi to the Lower Dan Tian, how to strengthen the Qi in the Dan Tian, and also how to apply the Qi for Jing. Externally, all of these styles typically emphasize the head being upright, the neck firm, the back arched, the shoulders loose, the waist and hips relaxed, and the anus movements coordinated. All of these criteria are very similar to those of Taijiquan. White Crane is therefore considered to be a "soft-hard" style: it is soft like Taiji, while the Jing can be as strong as a tiger's. In addition, all of the Crane styles focus on training the root and on stepping according to the theory of the five phases (i.e., metal, wood, water, fire, and earth).(*8)

Even though the basic theory is the same for all of the styles, each one of them has its own special emphasis and unique theory of training. Sleeping Crane (Su He), which is also called Ancestral Crane (Zong He) or Trembling Crane (Zhan He), specializes in the manifestation of Jing (i.e., martial power which is the manifestation of muscular power energized by Qi). It is called Sleeping Crane because it imitates the calmness and quiet of the crane. When the opportunity and timing are right, it attacks suddenly. Therefore, it emphasizes defense as offense. It is also called Ancestral Style because it is believed to carry out most of the teachings of the ancestor of the style. Finally, it is called Trembling Crane because it imitates the shaking or trembling power (Zhan Dou Jing) of the crane. After a rainfall, cranes can be seen shaking water off their bodies with a quick movement. The crane techniques used in this book are drawn from this style.

The Shouting Crane specializes in using the palm for striking, and also uses shouting while fighting. This style uses the palms like the crane's wings, as well as the sounds which cranes emit in the evening or the early morning. It is believed that the crane's cries can be heard miles away because they have very strong Qi in the Dan Tian. Shouting Crane style therefore emphasizes sinking the Qi and building it up in the Dan Tian.

The Eating Crane specializes in attacking with the beak. The movements are very agile and light, and speed is crucial in executing a successful technique.

Finally, the Flying Crane (Fei He) imitates the Crane's jumping and flying while at the same time using the wings to strike the opponent. Sounds are also often used in this style.

Long Fist (Changquan) means "long range" fighting style. The words Long Fist were first found in the document "Wu Pian" written by Tang Shun during the Ming dynasty (1368-1644 A.D.). He said, "When the distance is urgently short, use short strikes, and if far away, then use Long Fist."(*8,*9) From this, you can see that the meaning of the term Long Fist is "long range." At that time, Long Fist styles included Song Taizu Thirty-Two Long Fist and also the Wen Family's Seventy-Two Moving Sequences.

From the Qing dynasty to the present, more Long Fist styles have been created. Typical ones are: Tong Bei Quan (Long Arm Fist), Pi Gua (Chopping Diagram), Fan Zi (Flying Body), Cuo Jiao (Stepping Foot), Yan Qing (a personal name), Ying Zhua (Eagle Claw), Ba Ji (Eight Extremities), Tang Lang (Praying Mantis), Liu He (Six Combinations), Cha Quan (Cha Family Style), Hua Quan (Hua Mountain Style), Di Tang (Ground Style), Mei Hua (Plum Flower), Taizu (an emperor's name from the Song Dynasty), and many others.(*9)

This survey is meant only to give you a general idea of the history of these two styles. Since there are no documents giving an official history, we cannot be sure of exactly what happened.

1-3. Foundations of the White Crane and Long Fist Martial Styles

Before we discuss the foundation and strategy of White Crane and Long Fist fighting, we would first like to talk about general fighting tactics.

In Chinese martial arts it is said: "First, bravery; second, strength; and third, Gongfu" (Yi Dan, Er Li, San Gongfu).(*10) This means that the first requirement in a fight situation is that you must be brave enough to deal with the problem. If you are afraid, your mind will be scattered and you will not have control of your body. In this case, how can you defend yourself? Therefore, if you want to learn how to fight well, you must first learn courage and bravery. As mentioned earlier, courage comes from understanding and preparation. When you understand that fighting is the only way out, you will be prepared both psychologically and physically. Many people who have practiced martial arts for years are still unable to defend themselves in a street fight. This is not because they do not have good martial techniques, it is simply because they have never encountered a situation like that before, and they are not prepared for it psychologically.

Even if you are perfectly prepared mentally, you still must have enough strength to execute your decisions. Many people who have the courage to fight lack the strength to do so effectively. On the other hand, many people who are very strong and brave can fight effectively even though they have no techniques. When two equally prepared persons fight, then the one with the greater mastery of techniques will win. The person who has trained properly will also have developed confidence during his or her training, and will have learned fighting strategy. You can see that effective self-defense requires first, mental preparation; second, power; and finally, techniques.

Now, you may ask, "What about people who are weak, how can they defend themselves?" People who have little strength have to train techniques more intensively to compensate for their weakness. In the Chinese martial arts it is said: "First, speed; second, techniques; and third, strength." The reason for this is very simple. There are many areas where the human body can be injured easily to immobilize an opponent or limit his ability to fight. For example, little strength is needed to inflict serious damage to the eyes, nose, throat, solar plexus, groin, and the shins. You can even cause death in some of these areas if you inflict significant injury.

When you are in a situation which is going to develop into a fight, you must immediately realize that either you or your attacker is going to be a victim. If you do not want to be the victim, then you must prepare yourself to do your worst to the opponent. It is said: "If you are merciful to your enemy, you are cruel to yourself." It is extremely important that you understand this and take it to heart. If you fail to do this, then you are depriving yourself of the mental preparation which is absolutely necessary for defending yourself.

In China, there are many styles which are suitable for weak people who wish to defend themselves. However, in order to make the techniques effective, speed is most important. You must be able to reach your opponent's weak areas with such speed and accuracy that he does not have much chance to defend himself. This implies that in order to execute the techniques fast and skillfully, you should emphasize only a few effective ones and practice them until you can do them very proficiently. Learning a lot of techniques that you cannot use is equivalent to learning nothing. Always remember: **MASTERING A FEW EFFECTIVE TECHNIQUES IS BETTER THAN LEARNING MANY INEFFECTIVE TECHNIQUES**.

Among the many styles of Chinese martial arts, White Crane and Long Fist are two of the most efficient and effective. Each has its own unique theory and strategy. For example, White Crane specializes in hand techniques, and is therefore good for defending against short range attacks; while Long Fist emphasizes kicking, and is best at long range fighting. To help you understand these two styles, we will now summarize some of their characteristics.

White Crane:
The crane is a weak animal, with little strength to use in fighting. However, when necessary, it can defend itself very efficiently. A crane defending itself relies on only three things: its ability to jump around, the breaking power of its wings, and the pecking of its beak. Jumping around is used to dodge an attack and also to approach the opponent for an attack. When a crane uses its wings to strike, it can generate enough power to break a large branch. The key to this kind of power is speed. Remember that even though water is soft, if it is squirted out fast enough, it can be used in place of a knife in surgical operations. Finally, the accuracy with which a crane can quickly peck with its beak is very effective in attacking vital areas. This is a survival skill in another way, because the crane uses its beak to catch fish.

Based on this description, we can summarize a few characteristics of the Crane style:

1. Hands are more important than feet. When a crane uses either its beak or wings to fight, it must be stable, so it doesn't have much ability to kick. Therefore, in both defense and attack, the hands are used as either wings or beaks, while the legs are of lesser importance and are used only in coordination with the hand techniques. The key to successful defense and attack is the speed and accuracy of the hands.

2. Defense is used as an offense. Because the crane is a weak animal, it has to use defense as its offense. It must be calm, quiet, steady, alert, and ready to attack. When the opportunity comes and the timing is right, the attack is executed in the blink of an eye. The strategy of the crane is therefore to protect itself and wait for the opportunity to attack.

3. Fighting is done at short and middle range. Because the crane uses defense as an offense, it must be expert at fighting from short and middle range. When the opponent moves from long range to middle range, the Crane stylist will jump to short range to attack with the hands in coordination with limited kicking techniques. After the attack, the Crane stylist will jump back immediately to avoid being grabbed. Since the crane is a weak animal, if it is grabbed it will have no chance to escape. To deal with this problem, Crane stylists learn Qin Na (seize and control) techniques to deal with being grabbed.

4. Speed is more important than power. Although the power of an attack is considered important, it is not as important as speed in Crane training. In order to make the techniques effective, you must be able to dodge in and out and attack with your hands or legs very quickly. In order to increase effectiveness, accurate attacks to vital areas are also emphasized.

To conclude, Crane training focuses on keeping the proper distance with jumping or moving, and speed and accuracy in attacks to vital areas.

Long Fist:

1. **Kicks are more important than hands.** Long Fist was developed in northern China. Generally speaking, northern Chinese people are taller and have longer legs than southern Chinese people, so they take advantage of this and emphasize kicking. In addition, legs are generally stronger than arms. In Long Fist, there is a proverb: "Hands are like two doors, raise the legs to kick the opponent" (Shou Shi Lian San Men, Tai Jiao Jiu Da Ren).(*11) This means that the hands are used only for blocking, like doors or gates which are used to stop an invasion. Once you have blocked, you immediately kick the opponent.

2. **Defense and offense are equally important.** There are many northern styles that are considered Long Fist styles. Among them, some emphasize offense and use the offense as defense. They claim that the best defense is a strong offense. Continuous attacks are used to put the opponent on the defensive so that he does not have an opportunity to attack you. Other styles, however, believe that both defense and offense are equally important. Regardless of which view they hold, all the Long Fist styles are relatively more aggressive than the Crane style.

3. **Emphasis on middle and long range fighting.** Since kicking is used more than hand techniques, most of the fighting strategies and techniques reflect this. This means that Long Fist stylists favor middle and long range distances so that they can execute kicking techniques more efficiently. When a Long Fist fighter encounters an opponent, he usually keeps at long range where he is able to take advantage of his kicking ability, and where the opponent cannot use hand techniques. Occasionally, the Long Fist fighter will close to middle range so that he can use his kicks, but quickly retreat to long range once he has completed his technique.

4. **Speed is more important than power.** Since it takes a longer time to execute a kick from long range, the speed at which the fighter approaches his opponent and the speed of the kick are critical. In addition, since kicks are already more powerful than hand attacks, whenever a kick is successful it usually inflicts more damage than hand attacks can. Do not be deceived into thinking that power is not important in a fight. When two proficient martial artists encounter each other, if their speed and techniques are equal, then power will become the critical, decisive factor. However, it usually takes a long time to develop a great deal of power, so in a street fight you will probably not encounter a proficient martial artist. Therefore, in most self defense situations power is not a critical factor.

To summarize, the Long Fist stylist emphasizes the proper "distance" for the kicking techniques, the "speed" of advancing and withdrawing, and the "aggressive" execution of techniques.

You can see from the discussion in this chapter that, because of the different emphasis and characteristics of the Crane and Long Fist styles, it is wise to take advantage of both, combining them into a more effective and efficient self-defense art.

References

(*1). 滿招損，謙受益
(*2). 孔子曰："三人行，必有我師。"
(*3). 人上有人，天上有天。
(*4). 竹高愈躬
(*5). 敬人者，人恒敬之。
(*6). "Historical Drama of Shaolin," by Shao Yu-Sheng. "少林演義，" 少餘生編著。
(*7). "Qian Long Visits South of the River," Author unknown. "乾隆下江南，" 作者不詳。
(*8). "Zhongguo Wushu," by Kang Ge-Wu, 1990. "中國武術實用大全，" 康戈武編著。
(*9). "Terms of Wushu," by Ma You-Qing, 1985. "中國武術詞語手冊，" 馬有清編著。
(*10). 一胆，二力，三功夫。
(*11). 手是兩扇門，抬脚就打人。

Chapter 2
Psychology and Strategy of Self-Defense

2-1. Psychology of Self-Defense

This book is designed to prepare you to defend yourself, and it will therefore focus only on defensive techniques and strategy. If you would like to become a proficient martial artist and learn offensive techniques, you should either join a martial arts school or refer to other professional martial arts books.

In this chapter we will first analyze the psychology of the attacker and the defender. In the second section, we will discuss strategies and rules for when you have to defend yourself.

Psychology of the Attacker:

Before we analyze the attacker's psychology, let us first ponder why one society and culture can produce so many different types of people. It would seem that the strongest influence in how an individual turns out lies in how he or she grew up. When a child is born, it is completely pure and innocent. How the child turns out mentally and physically is formalized during childhood. Let us consider a few of the reasons why some children turn into criminals.

A major cause of criminality is the family background, regardless of whether the specific problem is abuse, drugs and alcohol, neglect or poverty. I believe that more than 70% of the causes of criminal actions originated during the process of growing up in a family. The main cause is when the child grows up without love. This results in either an introverted child who hides all of its internal suffering and hate inside, or one who expressed its feelings externally, unconsciously trying to win attention. Such children normally hate the world and society. They believe that they have been treated unfairly, especially when they see other children leading happy lives.

A child may not receive love for many different reasons. Perhaps the parents cannot get along with each other; in such cases the child often feels ignored. In single parent families, or in families where both parents are working, the parents often do not have time for their children. A child in this situation will often feel that he is a victim of money and society.

Many children also receive bad influences from their parents, and grow up thinking that smoking, drinking, and gambling are normal habits.

Many people think that such situations occur only in poor families, but this is not true. Even in many well-to-do families parents are not available, or just do not pay enough attention when the children are confused about their lives and need someone to help them. Many parents are too involved in their social lives or jobs. Children in such families often commit crimes just to get attention.

When children lack the guidelines for their lives that they should receive from their parents, they will use their imagination, and they will search around and imitate other people. What they learn from school, TV, and movies occupies their minds. They may learn from textbooks that, in order to become a hero, they must kill or conquer other people. A child may decide that, in order to prove that he is a man and not afraid, he must follow the lead shown on TV and rob a bank. This offers not only excitement and mental satisfaction, but also the prospect of becoming rich. Or he may try to win self-respect by committing other crimes such as robbery or rape.

If someone attacks you, one or more of the following situations probably applies to them:

1. His family was not normal.
2. He is psychologically unbalanced, and probably despises himself.
3. There was a lack of love, lack of empathy or outright abuse during childhood.
4. He is trying to prove he is not a coward.
5. He is looking for mental satisfaction and stimulation.
6. He needs money. This can be for survival, drugs, or alcohol.
7. He desires respect and dignity. An easy way to win attention from parents, friends, or society is by committing a crime.

Next, imagine that you have that kind of background, and intend to commit a crime. What are you feeling? What are you thinking about? What is the psychology of a person who attacks other ?

1. HE IS VERY NERVOUS AND TENSE. The greatest satisfaction that committing a crime brings is probably excitement and stimulation. Right after a successful crime, many criminals are usually very stimulated, but also relaxed and feeling very gratified. It is the same feeling that anyone gets after completing a difficult task.

While committing the crime, they are therefore mentally very nervous and tense. Another group of assailants seem cold and almost emotionless but may be "revved up" and very vigilant.

2.   HE WANTS TO FINISH THE JOB AS QUICKLY AS POSSIBLE. Because he is tense and nervous, he wants to finish the job as soon as possible, especially since he knows that the longer it takes, the greater the chances are of getting caught.

3.   HE DOESN'T WANT TO TALK. Since the attacker is probably psychologically unbalanced, he will usually feel uneasy inside. He does not want to talk with you and expose feelings such as fear or guilt. I believe that everyone, including the worst career criminal, knows deep inside what is right and what is wrong.

4.   HE IS AFRAID OF BRIGHT AREAS. When someone attacks you he will usually avoid well-lit areas where you can see his face and where other people can notice what is happening. Another possible reason is that he does not want you to see his face because he cannot hide how guilty he is feeling.

5.   HE IS AFRAID OF CROWDS. Almost all attackers are afraid of crowds because they can interfere with the crime.

6.   HE IS AFRAID OF DRAWING ATTENTION. Criminals dislike noise or anything else that will draw attention when they are committing a crime, because it increases the likelihood that the crime will be interrupted (Exceptions to this point include gang actions where display is often desired).

7.   HE LIKES TO STAY CLOSE TO THE VICTIM. An experienced attacker wants to stay close to you so that he can grab and control you, or inflict injury. In addition, it is usually easier to terrify the victim at close range.

8.   HE LIKES TO FORCE THE VICTIM INTO A CORNER OR AGAINST A WALL. Attackers frequently like to force the victim into a corner or against a wall so that they cannot escape. This is also more frightening for the victim because it limits the options.

9.   HE EXPECTS MOST VICTIMS TO BE AFRAID AND TO SURRENDER. Attackers expect that most victims will be afraid and surrender. It is in fact true that most people who are attacked do not resist or even fight back.

10. HE IS AFRAID THE VICTIM MIGHT BE PREPARED BOTH MENTALLY AND PHYSICALLY. If an attacker discovers that the intended victim is prepared mentally and physically, he will realize that his job has suddenly become more difficult, and he will usually go off and find an easier victim. He will want to avoid trouble and the risk of getting arrested. Note, however, that the intended victim must truly be prepared; an empty semblance of readiness or half-hearted preparation may be provocative rather than deterrent.

11. HIS MIND IS IN CONFLICT. For the non-hardened criminal, such as one who commits muggings just to survive, the conflict is often like that seen in gambling. One part of his mind knows that what he is doing is wrong and shameful, but another part enjoys the excitement and mental satisfaction. Normally, his emotional mind has control of his being before and during the crime. However, once the excitement is over, his wisdom mind brings his guilty feelings to the surface. Hardened criminals, in contrast, may be capable of feeling neither guilt nor remorse.

Psychology of a Victim:

What is the reaction of a victim when he or she is physically attacked? It is important that you think about this, so that if you are ever in a situation where you may be attacked, you will not act like a victim. If you react in an unexpected way, you will upset the attacker's mental balance and improve your chances. People who are attacked often react in the following ways:

1. YOU ARE STARTLED, AFRAID, AND IN SHOCK. When you are attacked, you fear that you may be hurt or even killed. You are also startled and in shock, and do not know how to react. You would like to run, but you can't. You would also like to yell, but you can't make a sound.

2. YOU FEEL TOTALLY ALONE. The second thought in your mind is probably the hope that someone has noticed what is going on and is either coming to help you or else calling the police.

3. YOU ARE WONDERING HOW TO ESCAPE. You lack confidence in your ability to defend yourself, and wish that you had learned some self defense techniques and strategy. You may feel more helpless than you are.

In the next section we will discuss strategies of self defense based on the issues raised in this section.

2-2. Defense Strategies

Before we discuss defense strategies, you should know that the best strategy for your safety is keeping away from dangerous situations. You should always keep away from dark areas and alleys; when in doubt, walk in the middle of the street away from parked cars. If possible, always walk among crowds or at least find some companions. Invest in a taxicab. Trust your instincts and don't be embarrassed to run for fear it will look silly. Simply use your common sense and avoid situations which offer attackers an opportunity. However, should you ever be attacked, then you need to have strategies for defending yourself.

Buying and reading this book is one kind of preparation; another kind is an internal process of thoughtful consideration of your own values and mental rehearsal. You will learn some very effective skills if you read, practice and understand the lessons here, but with skill comes responsibility. You must think through the implications of your actions, now, while reading, before you have to act in reality.

How do you **yourself** feel about acting violently toward someone else, even someone who intends to hurt you? About injuring someone, perhaps permanently? Do you agree that someone who assaults you has broken the social contract to a great enough degree that he has — knowingly or not — accepted the risks of violence, including any damage inflicted by you in self-defense? That by attacking you without restraint, he has forfeited his right to your restraint in counterattacking? Coming to your own terms with these questions is an absolutely essential part of your preparation: meditate on these issues in privacy, discuss them with friends, do not ignore them. Your consideration of these questions is the foundation of the proper mental attitude required for rejecting the victim role.

The most important point you should realize is: **DO NOT FIGHT UNLESS IT IS NECESSARY**. If you are able to run toward a crowd, you should do so immediately once you realize that you are being threatened. However, if you cannot run, make sure you understand what the situation actually is. If the person is only looking for money, your best bet is probably to give it to him. If giving him money will get you out of the situation with no injuries, why take a chance? Simply offer him some money and let him walk away, and then report him to the police.

1.   **REMAIN CALM AND CONFIDENT.** When you are nervous and scared, you cannot remain calm and you may not be able to handle the situation. You must first recognize that if you are afraid and act like a victim, you diminish your chances of dealing with the situation successfully. You must face your attacker with bravery and confidence. Approach the situation with your wisdom mind instead of with your emotional mind. This is easier to do if you have already prepared yourself physically and mentally for the confrontation.

2.   When the situation occurs, try to **KEEP THE ATTACKER AT LONG RANGE**. You should not allow him to close in to short range, because you will not be able to watch him as clearly, and you will have less time to react. If your attacker has entered middle range and you can kick, you should do so immediately. This will prevent him from closing to short range where he will be able to punch or grab you.

3.   **WHEN YOU NEED TO ACT, ACT FAST.** If your assessment of the situation is that avoiding the fight is impossible — and you should trust your instincts about this — take immediate action. If you hesitate you may lose the chance. For example, while at long range you may pick up a brick or rock or take off your belt to fight with. If the attacker steps forward, punch his face or attack his shin or groin with a fast kick. All of these actions tell your opponent that you are prepared mentally and will not be an easy victim. If possible make your move while the attacker is talking, since he is then in a slightly distracted state. Many individuals while speaking avoid eye contact so as not to invite interruption; if your attacker looks away or even closes his

eyes while making a point, strike then without warning.

4.   YOUR MIND SHOULD BE FIRM. If you are uncertain or confused, the attacker will have a chance to overcome you both mentally and psychologically. However, if your mind is firm and you are psychologically prepared, you will be able to dominate the situation. When your mind is firm, you send your attacker the message that you are ready to deal with him. **DO NOT HESITATE** to carry out any decision. In a fight, either you or the attacker will be the victim.

5.   IMMEDIATELY MOVE TO AN ADVANTAGEOUS POSITION. When you are still at long range, you should immediately move to a brighter area, the brighter the better, so that you can see his actions clearly. Attackers usually don't like well-lit areas. There is also the concern that other people may see what is going on. You should also move behind a post, a garbage can, or near anything which you can use to better your chances. It is also better to have your back to the light or the sun so that it doesn't interfere with your vision.

6.   AVOID BEING FORCED INTO A CORNER OR AGAINST A WALL. When you are at long range, beware of being forced into a corner or against a wall. This limits many of your options for defending yourself, and also prevents you from retreating if necessary. The best way of keeping away from corners and walls is to keep circling your opponent.

7.   TALK TO THE ATTACKER. When you are at long range from your opponent, try to talk to him calmly. Some authorities suggest talking very abstractly about how violence is not a useful solution, how there must be other ways to deal with situations, and so on. It is best to speak in an absolutely flat, monotonous tone while keeping your face as mask-like and expressionless as your voice. This approach can create a kind of hypnotic state which is to your advantage. If you get your attacker talking you may learn what his intentions are and what kind of a person he is. More importantly, you may be able to calm him down and make him less excited. You may persuade him to give up his intention. Most important of all, if you can talk to the attacker with a confident and calm mind, you will give him the message that you are prepared for him and will not be an easy victim.

8.   ATTRACT PEOPLE'S ATTENTION. Whenever you can, you should make as much noise as possible and move toward lights and people. Remember, this is only possible if you keep a good distance from the attacker.

9.   DO NOT FIGHT AGAINST A GUN. Unless you are absolutely certain that he is going to kill you, you should never take the chance of fighting a gun. It is almost impossible to fight against a gun if you are even a few yards away from it. He can pull the trigger much faster than you can reach him. It is especially dangerous when the attacker is nervous, because any unexpected action may cause him to pull the trigger. When the distance is short, however, if you know what you are doing and your reactions are very fast, then you may have a chance to disarm him. In such a situation, you should not hesitate to attack vital areas such as the eyes, groin, or throat.

This chapter is meant to only offer some general suggestions on how you may prepare yourself mentally to deal with an attack. There are many other situations which may arise, and you just have to use your judgment and common sense. As long as you remain calm and react quickly, I believe you will be able to handle most problems. The most important factor, however, is developing the confidence to handle threatening situations, and this is best accomplished by learning the defense strategy and techniques which will be introduced in the next two chapters. It is best if you can practice with partners, simulating situations that might occur.

Chapter 3
Defense Against Barehand Attack

3-1. Introduction

Generally speaking, it is easier to defend against an unarmed attacker than it is against an armed one. We will therefore present defenses against an unarmed attacker in this chapter, and in the next chapter we will introduce defenses that can be used against an attacker armed with a short knife. Since much of the basic theory and techniques are the same regardless of whether the attacker is armed or not, this chapter serves as a preliminary training course for the next chapter.

Self defense techniques can be divided into long range, middle range, and short range techniques, and so we will organize our discussion accordingly.

In addition to the strategy and techniques discussed in this chapter, the most important requirement of a successful defense is a calm mind, because this allows you to evaluate the situation accurately and use common sense. When you are confronted by someone, you are facing not only a possible physical fight, but also a psychological battle between you and your opponent. If you are calm and willing to accept the challenge, you have already won the battle psychologically. This mental/emotional victory may enable you to avoid having to actually fight the opponent physically. Remember: **THE BEST FIGHT IS NO FIGHT**.

In order to make your defense effective, you must find a partner and practice the techniques in this chapter until you are confident. Just reading this book will give you some strategic concepts, but it cannot guarantee your ability to defend yourself physically.

3-2. Basic Training

In this section we will introduce some of the basic training which is required for the fast and effective execution of a technique.

Figure 3-1.

Figure 3-2.

You should practice as much as possible.

Sense of Distance:

The first thing you need to develop is a sense of distance. Different distances between you and your opponent require different strategies and techniques. Generally speaking, Chinese martial arts use three ranges: long range (Chang Ju), middle range (Zhong Ju), and short range (Duan Ju). Long range is when you or your opponent cannot punch or kick without first moving forward (Figure 3-1). Both parties are relatively safe, since any attempt to attack can be clearly seen. It is therefore not easy to attack successfully at this range.

Middle range is the distance at which either you or your opponent can reach the other person with a kick without taking a step (Figure 3-2). At this range a punch usually cannot reach the opponent unless you step or hop forward into short range. This range is more danger-ous for both sides than long range since you can be kicked, and so you have to pay particular attention to the opponent's legs.

Figure 3-3.

Figure 3-4.

Finally, short range is the distance where you and your opponent can punch or grab each other (Figure 3-3). Without question, this range is the most dangerous. In this range you must move fast and either attack or withdraw to long range.

You and your partner can develop a sense of the different ranges by standing at long range from each other and trying to touch each other's forehead or chest (Figure 3-4). When you sense your opponent moving forward, immediately step or hop back or to the sides, and do not allow him to get any closer. The more you practice, the more you will develop your sense of distance. The goal is to practice until you can maintain whatever distance you desire without thinking about it.

Circling:

If you cannot move quickly toward light and people, then circle your attacker. Circling is a strategy for putting your opponent at an angle which is disadvantageous for his attack, and which allows you to attack him through his empty door (Kong Men). An empty

Figure 3-5.

Figure 3-6.

Figure 3-7.

door is an angle through which you can attack your opponent easily. When you practice, if your partner tries to touch you with his right hand or foot, simply circle to his left (Figure 3-5). This puts him into a position where it is difficult for him to follow up with a second attack. If he attacks with his left hand or foot, you circle to his right. This will force him to circle with you, and will make it easier for you to defend yourself.

Circling also helps you avoid being channeled into a corner or against a wall. You can practice this with your partner by having him try to channel you into a corner or against the wall while you try to circle him and stay at long range (Figures 3-6 and 3-7). You will

Figure 3-8.

discover that it is not an easy task unless you keep in practice with your speed and faking movements.

Intercepting a Hand Attack:

After you have developed your sense of distance and an ability to circle, you should learn some of the basic intercepting techniques. It is said: "A successful interception is 80% of the counterattack." This means that when you intercept correctly and accurately, you place your opponent in a position where it is difficult for him to defend against your counterattack.

As you are intercepting an attack you should pay attention to your opponent's entire body, and not restrict your attention to the attacking limb (Figure 3-8). This will let you see any follow-up technique, and perhaps even prevent one.

We will now introduce three basic White Crane intercepting drills for use against a hand attack. We will leave kick interceptions for later when we discuss defenses against kicks.

1.   Repelling:

When someone attacks you, intercept it with either forearm and repel it to the side. You may repel a punch either to your left (Figure 3-9) or to your right (Figure 3-10), depending upon which technique you want to counterattack with.

To practice with a partner, simply try to touch each other's chest from various distances while intercepting and repelling the other person's attack (Figure 3-11). The more you practice, the easier and the more natural your intercepting will become.

2.   Covering:

When someone attacks you, use either forearm to intercept and cover to the side. You may cover to your left (Figure 3-12) or to your right (Figure 3-13), depending upon the situation and technique.

When you practice with a partner, simply try to touch each other's chest from various distances while intercepting and covering

Figure 3-9.

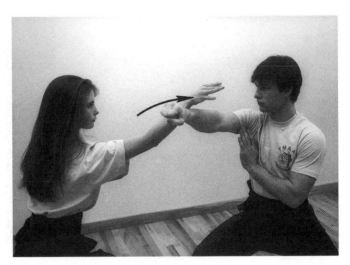

Figure 3-10.

Figure 3-11.

Figure 3-12.

Figure 3-13.

your partner's attacks with your forearm (Figure 3-14). The more you practice, the easier and more natural your intercepting will become.

3. Low Block:

This intercepting technique is used against a punch to the lower part of the body. When someone attacks your abdomen with his hand, intercept it and lead it to the side with your forearm. You may block the punch and lead it to your left (Figure 3-15) or to your right (Figure 3-16) depending on the situation.

When you practice with a partner, simply try to touch each other's stomach from various distances while defending yourself. The more you practice, the easier and the more natural it will become.

Once you have mastered these three interceptions, practice against a wide variety of punches until you can intercept all of them with the proper technique and distance.

Figure 3-14.

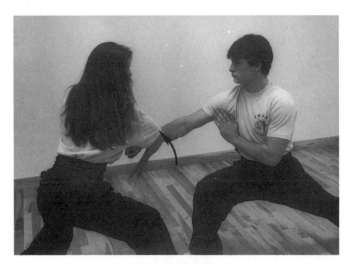

Figure 3-15.

Figure 3-16.

Figure 3-17.

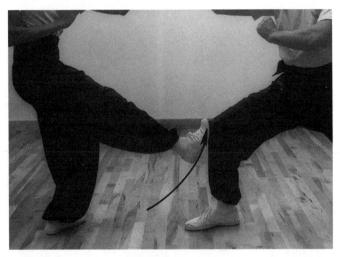

Figure 3-18.

Punching Drill:

Speed is the most important key to winning a fight. You must develop both the speed at which you intercept techniques and the speed and accuracy of your punches. You also need to develop a certain amount of power in your punches. This is something that you can practice anywhere and anytime. Simply imagine that you are punching someone, and punch him with speed and power. You can also punch targets like leaves on a tree, you can hang up a ping pong ball on a string and use it as a target, or anything else you can think of. A punching bag is a good choice for developing power.

Kicking:

Generally speaking, high kicks are dangerous to use since you expose your groin to attack. We will therefore focus only on those low kicks which are fast, powerful, effective, safe, and easy to learn.

The first kick uses the ball of the foot to attack your opponent's shin or kneecap (Figures 3-17 and 3-18). You can practice on a kicking bag or on a post covered with a pad or wrapped with a rug.

Figure 3-19.

Figure 3-20.

Practice kicking to the height of your shin or kneecap. First practice kicking while standing in place (Figure 3-19), and then learn how to hop forward and kick (Figures 3-20 and 3-21), and then immediately hop back (Figure 3-22).

The second kick uses the heel to attack the shin or knee (Figure 3-23). The third kick uses the toes or the heel to kick the groin (Figure 3-24). The fourth kick uses the side of your foot to attack the shin or knee (Figure 3-25). The fifth uses the heel to attack the abdomen (Figure 3-26). Finally, the sole of your foot can be used to attack the side of your opponent's calf (Figure 3-27). You can practice all of these kicks the same way you practiced the first one against a kicking bag,

Figure 3-21.

Figure 3-22.

Figure 3-23.

Figure 3-24.

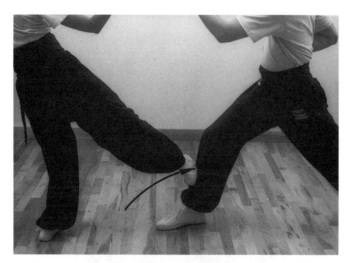

Figure 3-25.

Figure 3-26.

Figure 3-27.

Figure 3-28.

post, or tree to develop speed, power, and accuracy (Figure 3-28). If you have a kicking bag, you should also practice kneeing the bag at a right angle to develop speed and power (Figure 3-29).

3-3. Techniques

In a fight, if your opponent is at middle or long range you cannot reach him with a punch, so you should rely on kicks. Even at middle range, where you can punch the opponent if you step or hop forward, it is still better to rely on kicks as much as possible since they are much more powerful and effective than punches. Kicking also helps to keep your opponent from getting close to you.

Figure 3-29.

Once the opponent closes to short range, however, use both punches and short range kicks.

The best targets are the eyes, nose, throat, stomach, groin, and shins. However, only attack the eyes, throat, and groin when you are in great danger, since attacking these areas can cause the most damage. The easiest way to stop an attacker is to hit him in the nose or the shin. Punching the nose will cause extreme pain and tears. If your opponent continues to attack you, punch his nose again. The second time will immobilize him easily. Kicking the shin will interfere with your opponent's ability to walk or kick. Its most valuable effect, however, is that it prevents your opponent from chasing you when you run away.

In order for your techniques and strategies to work effectively, you must practice them constantly until you are very fast, powerful, and accurate. This will also give you the confidence you need to actually defend yourself if the need arises. Practicing with a partner is very important. Once you have developed these skills, you must learn to build up your fighting spirit so that you will not be afraid, and your mind will be firm and clear. Then you should be able to handle any situation comfortably.

Next, we will introduce some easily trained techniques for use against an attacker at long range, middle range, and short range.

Long Range:
When your opponent is at long range, if you do not have other options such as running away or toward people, then your best strategy for maintaining the distance is to circle your opponent. Circling

Figure 3-30.

Figure 3-31.

can also help you avoid being forced into a corner or against a wall. We will now introduce some practical techniques which you may use while you are circling your opponent or drawing away from him.

1.   Kicking:
    When you and your opponent are at long range, it is usually easier and safer to kick, rather than use hand techniques. As we mentioned earlier, low kicks are the most powerful and effective ones. Those fancy high kicks you see in movies need special training, and they are not very practical because you expose your groin (Figure 3-30). Low kicks are faster, and your stance is much more stable when you use them. The following are some of the effective kicks which you should learn.

Technique #1:
    The first kick uses the heel or the ball of the foot to kick the opponent's shin (Figure 3-31) or kneecap (Figure 3-32). Hop forward, kick, and retreat to long range immediately (Figures 3-33 and 3-34). You

Figure 3-32.

Figure 3-33.

Figure 3-34.

Figure 3-35.

Figure 3-36.

may use the same kicks when your opponent is stepping forward toward you (Figure 3-35). The kicks should be firm, accurate, and fast.

Technique #2:

Sometimes you may find that it is more convenient to use the side of your foot to kick the shin (Figure 3-36) or knee. As with the previous kick, you should hop forward and kick and then hop backward to long range again as soon as possible.

Technique #3:

The groin is the easiest area to injure. When you kick the groin, use the top of the toes (Figure 3-37) or the ball of the foot (Figure 3-38). Kick the shin the same way. After kicking, retreat as quickly as possible.

When you use any of these low kicks, you will often bring the opponent's attention for a moment to his legs (Figure 3-39). If you notice this happening, immediately punch him in the nose and then

Figure 3-37.

Figure 3-38.

Figure 3-39.

Figure 3-40.

Figure 3-41.

retreat (Figure 3-40). The best strategy when attacking is to keep changing your focus from his upper body to his lower body and legs.

2. Belt Techniques:
Technique #1:

If you have a leather belt with a metal buckle, then take it off immediately (as long as your pants won't drop). Belts are excellent weapons. If you coordinate the belt with your kicking, you can keep your opponent at long range and defend yourself quite easily.

When you use the belt do not swing it, because it can be caught too easily (Figure 3-41). Instead, snap it. Snapping lets you attack very quickly, and it also withdraws the belt immediately so that your opponent can't grab it. Always aim at the opponent's face, especially the eyes, to distract his attention - this gives you a chance to kick his legs or groin (Figure 3-42). You can also snap at his groin (Figure 3-43), however, this has a few disadvantages. First, the groin is usually somewhat protected by the pants. Second, snapping lower is

Figure 3-42.

Figure 3-43.

harder and less accurate, and the groin is a smaller target than the face. Third, your opponent can protect his groin easily with one hand, and still be able to attack you. He does not have this option when you attack his face, because if he puts a hand up to guard his face he also blocks his vision. Despite this, the groin is sometimes a good target, and it is harder for the opponent to catch the belt.

If you have practiced snapping the belt enough to be comfortable with it, then attack with the buckle end so that you can inflict more injury (Figure 3-44). However, if you are not skillful at using the belt, then you should not use the buckle end because it tends to bounce back and is hard to control.

3.   Using Bricks, Stones, or other Objects:
Technique #1:

Whenever you have the chance, pick up a brick, stone, or any small object which you can use for defense or attack. If you can, pick up two objects, so if you drop or throw one, you still have the other.

Figure 3-44.

Figure 3-45.

These objects can be thrown at the opponent's face to give you a chance to kick him (Figure 3-45). When you throw the object, you must be firm, powerful, and fast. Also, don't just throw the object right away; fake him a few times and look for an opening. Once you have an opportunity, however, don't hesitate. Hit him at once and don't feel guilty about it. Remember that if you don't hurt him, he is going to hurt you.

Middle Range:

When you are at middle range, you are in a more urgent situation and you don't have time to pick up anything around you or take off your belt. Therefore, you must act immediately. Either withdraw to long range or kick him right away. Staying at this range too long is dangerous.

When you are at middle range, your opponent will either kick you or step forward to punch or grab you whenever he has a chance. Next, we will introduce some defensive techniques for this situation.

Figure 3-46.

Figure 3-47.

1. Techniques Against Kicks:

Defending against a kick is not as easy as defending against a punch, because a kick is more powerful and can inflict greater injury. This is especially so if the attacker has some training in kicking. It is very difficult to intercept a kick accurately and successfully without proper training. We therefore urge beginners to simply dodge away and not try to intercept.

Technique #1:

The simplest way to defend against a kick is to dodge away or to retreat. If you are dodging, always dodge to the empty door so that you can punch your opponent (Figure 3-46) or kick him (Figure 3-47). Do not bother to block unless you are very skillful. You can also dodge backward (Figure 3-48), though this gives your opponent a chance to kick again or punch. When you dodge to the side, your opponent has to change his direction in order to kick again, but when you withdraw straight back it is very easy for him to hop

Figure 3-48.

Figure 3-49.

forward for another kick or punch (Figure 3-49).

Technique #2:

Low kicks are usually very difficult to block or intercept simply because they are harder to reach with your hand. However, they can be dodged very easily. If you are in an urgent situation and cannot dodge or retreat, then you may intercept a low kick such as one to your groin by simply withdrawing your front leg and intercepting the kick with the outside of your calf (Figure 3-50). When you intercept, at the same time punch your opponent in the face (Figure 3-51). If the opponent is too far away for an effective punch, you may still use your right leg to kick his groin after your block (Figure 3-52).

Technique #3:

If your opponent's kick is aimed at your stomach, you may again dodge to his empty door. Alternatively, you may step backward slightly to an appropriate distance and scoop the kick upward (Figure 3-53). If you execute the technique correctly, you may lock

Figure 3-50.   Figure 3-51.

Figure 3-52.

your opponent's kicking leg in the air (Figure 3-54). This will allow you to kick his groin, knee, or shin (Figure 3-55).

Technique #4:

If your opponent kicks at you higher than your stomach, simply dodge to his empty door and kick his groin (Figure 3-56) or punch his nose (Figure 3-57). If he kicks higher than your chest, you can usually

Figure 3-53.

Figure 3-54.

Figure 3-55.

Figure 3-56.

Figure 3-57.

simply lean backward without blocking and use your foot to kick his groin (Figure 3-58). Your distance and timing must be accurate, or you may still be kicked. If possible, practice with a partner as much as possible. When your opponent kicks you, use both hands on his ankle to lift the leg upward (Figure 3-59), lean back (if necessary, step backward to the proper distance) and kick his groin (Figure 3-60). When you practice this with a partner, make sure his groin is well protected.

Next, we will introduce techniques for defense against a punch in middle range. You may use a takedown on your opponent or simply punch him as a counterattack.

Figure 3-58.

Figure 3-59.

Figure 3-60.

Figure 3-61.

2. Techniques for Taking Down or Striking:

At middle range, it is very common for an opponent to immediately charge forward and punch. Here are some techniques to defend against this by either taking him down or striking him. The purpose of taking an attacker down is to demonstrate to them that you are able to defend yourself. This will usually discourage them from attacking you further, and so the situation is resolved with no injuries on either side.

However, it is very important that you understand that it is much harder to take the opponent down than to just hit them. If you have trained enough so that you can take an attacker down, it usually means that you could hit them even more easily. In this section, we will include both options. Of course, you may also take your opponent down first, and then follow up with a strike while he is still on the ground.

Technique #1:

When your opponent steps forward to punch you, the safest and fastest way to avoid the attack is to step back or to the side without bothering to intercept his punch (Figure 3-61). While you are retreating or dodging to the side, you can also kick his shin, knee, or groin (Figure 3-62). In this case, while his mind is on attacking above with a short weapon (his arm), you are attacking below with a long weapon (your leg). To do this, your reaction must be fast and the techniques must be executed accurately and powerfully.

Technique #2:

When your opponent steps forward and attacks you with his right hand, dodge to his left and use your left forearm to repel his punch to his right (Figure 3-63). Immediately punch his face with your right hand (Figure 3-64) or kick his groin with your right leg (Figure 3-65).

Technique #3:

When your opponent punches you with his right hand, repel it to his right with your left forearm (Figure 3-66). At the same time,

Figure 3-62.

Figure 3-63.

Figure 3-64.

Figure 3-65.

Figure 3-66.

circle his neck with your right arm and press to his right, while placing your right leg behind his right leg (Figure 3-67). Then push your right arm down and use your right leg to sweep his right leg and take him down (Figure 3-68). You may also use your right hand to grab his throat, attack his face, or punch his stomach (Figure 3-69). If the distance is close, simply use your right elbow to strike the face or solar plexus (Figure 3-70).

Alternatively, after you have repelled the punch with your left arm, use your left hand to grab his right wrist and at the same time use your right forearm to lock and break his right elbow (Figure 3-71). You may then use your right foot to kick the inside of his right calf to make him fall (Figure 3-72). If the distance is appropriate, you can also knee his groin (Figure 3-73).

Technique #4:
When your opponent punches you with his right fist, intercept it with your right hand and push it to your left (Figure 3-74).

Figure 3-67.

Figure 3-68.

Figure 3-69.

Figure 3-70.

Figure 3-71.

Figure 3-72.

Figure 3-73.

Figure 3-74.

Immediately use your left hand to punch his lower ribs near the liver (Figure 3-75). Alternatively, you may use your left fist to punch his jaw (Figure 3-76).

If you desire to take him down, simply use your left arm to lock his neck while stepping your left leg behind his right leg (Figure 3-77). Finally, press your left arm downward while using your left leg to lock and sweep his right leg (Figure 3-78).

Alternatively, while you are using your left arm to press his throat and put him into a disadvantageous position (Figure 3-79), use your right arm to hook and lift his right knee (Figure 3-80). You may then throw him to your rear (Figure 3-81). You can also use

Figure 3-75.

Figure 3-76.

Figure 3-77.

Figure 3-78.

Figure 3-79.

Figure 3-80.

Figure 3-81.

Figure 3-82.

your right hand to grab or strike his groin instead (Figure 3-82).

Technique #5:

When your opponent attacks you with his right fist, use your right hand to cover to his right (Figure 3-83), immediately following with a backfist strike to his jaw or temple with your right fist (Figure 3-84). You may also simply use the edge of your right palm to chop his neck (Figure 3-85).

You may also use your right leg to kick the inside of his right shin (Figure 3-86). Alternatively, you may use your right hand to grab his hair and pull it down while using your right knee to attack his groin or stomach (Figure 3-87).

Technique #6:

When your opponent punches you with his right fist, use your right hand to repel the punch to the right, and at the same time grab his right wrist with your left hand (Figure 3-88). Immediately step behind his right leg with your right leg, while at the same time

Figure 3-83.

Figure 3-84.

Figure 3-85.

Figure 3-86.

Figure 3-87.

Figure 3-88.

Figure 3-89.

Figure 3-90.

pulling his right arm to his right side and downward (Figure 3-89). Finally, sweep your right leg backward and at the same time pull your opponent down (Figure 3-90).

Alternatively, after you have intercepted the opponent's right arm and pulled it down (Figure 3-89), you may immediately punch his temple or jaw with your right fist (Figure 3-91).

Technique #7:

When your opponent punches you with his right fist, repel it to the right with your right hand as you turn your body to the right, and at the same time seal his elbow with your left hand (Figure 3-92). Then lock his neck with your left arm while stepping your left leg behind his right leg (Figure 3-93). Finally, push him down while sweeping his right leg with your left leg (Figure 3-94).

Alternatively, you may simply strike his face with your left fist (Figure 3-95), or attack his throat or neck with your forearm (Figure 3-96).

Figure 3-91.

Figure 3-92.

Figure 3-93.

Figure 3-94.

Figure 3-95.

Figure 3-96.

Figure 3-97.

Figure 3-98.

Technique #8:

When your opponent punches you with his right fist, repel it with your right hand (Figure 3-97). Immediately grab his right wrist and pull it down while kicking his groin or shin with your right leg (Figure 3-98).

Technique #9:

When your opponent punches you with his right fist, repel it to your right with your right arm while covering his right elbow with your left hand (Figure 3-99). Immediately grab his jaw and head while stepping behind his right leg with your right leg (Figure 3-100). You may now break his neck or take him down by pressing downward while sweeping your right leg backward (Figure 3-101).

Short Range:

When you and your opponent are in short range, you are in an urgent situation. You must decide immediately whether to attack or withdraw. At this range you can be surprised by a sudden attack. If

Figure 3-99.

Figure 3-100.

Figure 3-101.

Figure 3-102.　　　　　　　Figure 3-103.

you decide not to attack, then you should step or jump back to long range and prepare for the next strategy or movement. However, if you decide to attack, you should attack immediately without hesitation.

In this section we will first discuss short range punching and kicking techniques. The main reason that the punching and kicking techniques are emphasized here is simply that they are easier to execute and more powerful than Qin Na control or takedown techniques. We will then introduce some Qin Na (seize and control) techniques which enable you to defend against a grabbing attack without harming the opponent. Of course, in order to execute these techniques successfully, you have to be more skillful and faster than your opponent. Remember that if your opponent is able to grab any part of your body, then he is close enough for you to punch or kick him. Punching and kicking are the safest and most effective way to defend yourself (after running away), while using Qin Na to control the attacker is a secondary method which you may choose to use when you feel quite confident of being able to handle him.

1. Punching and Kicking:
Technique #1:

Once your opponent has come into short range, immediately grab his clothes or arms with both hands and kick his shin with the ball or sole of your foot (Figure 3-102), or knee him in the groin (Figure 3-103). You can also grab his neck or hair to execute the same attacks (Figure 3-104).

Technique #2:

If your opponent tries to grab or punch you (Figure 3-105),

Figure 3-104.

Figure 3-105.

Figure 3-106.

Figure 3-107.

intercept his attack with one arm and repel it to the side while punching upward to his chin with your other fist (Figure 3-106). You can also punch his stomach (Figure 3-107) or groin (Figure 3-108).

Technique #3:

If your opponent is just out of range of a hooking punch to the

Figure 3-108.

Figure 3-109.

jaw, you can instead punch his nose, throat, or eyes while intercepting his attack with your other hand and repelling it to the side (Figures 3-109 and 3-110).

Technique #4:

When you are close enough, you should use elbow attacks as much as possible because they are much more powerful than hand attacks. For example, when your opponent tries to punch or grab you, intercept his arm with one hand (Figure 3-111), then step in and hook his neck with the same hand (Figure 3-112). Then hit him in the solar plexus with the elbow of the other arm (Figure 3-113).

Figure 3-110.

Figure 3-111.

Figure 3-112.

Technique #5:

If your opponent grabs you with both hands (Figure 3-114), repel both of his arms and grab them (or the front of his shirt), and then strike his nose with your forehead (Figure 3-115). Headbutts are usually quite unexpected, and you will be surprised at how easily this technique can be executed.

Technique #6:

If your opponent tries to attack or grab you with his left hand (Figure 3-116), repel it to the side with your right hand while simultaneously pushing his right shoulder or face with your left hand (Figure 3-117). Then immediately chop his neck with the edge of

Figure 3-113.

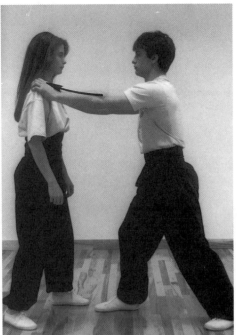

Figure 3-114.

Figure 3-115.

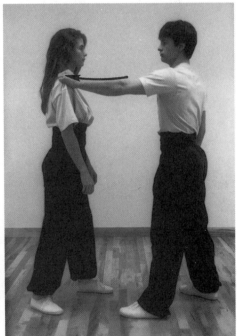

Figure 3-116.

your right hand (Figure 3-118). If your opponent uses both hands to grab you (Figure 3-119), you can execute a similar blocking and chopping technique with both hands simultaneously (Figure 3-120).

Technique #7:

When your opponent comes into a range where you can kick him

Figure 3-117.

Figure 3-118.

Figure 3-119.

Figure 3-120.

or even step on his toes with your heel (Figure 3-121), you should do so at once to bring his attention downward. This will make it easier for you to punch him in the head (Figure 3-122).

Technique #8:

This technique makes your opponent lose his balance, which

Figure 3-121.

Figure 3-122.

Figure 3-123.

Figure 3-124.

allows you to attack him safely. When your opponent tries to punch or grab you (Figure 3-123), quickly grab one or both arms and pull him down forcefully while stepping to the rear and side (Figure 3-124). Immediately kick him in the groin or chest while he is still off balance (Figure 3-125).

Figure 3-125.   Figure 3-126.

These simple techniques can give you some ideas on how to defend yourself, but you must practice them until you know them well and can adapt them to any situation. Things happen very quickly in short range, and you do not have much time to think. You must react automatically without hesitation. This will only happen if you practice a lot with a partner, going through all the possible variations of what may happen.

Next, we will introduce some Qin Na techniques which are useful against grabbing attacks. If you are interested in learning more Qin Na techniques, please refer to the YMAA book "Analysis of Shaolin Chin Na" and the videotape "Shaolin Chin Na."

2. Qin Na Against Grabbing Attacks:

It is very common for people to grab you once they are in short range. While the most effective way to defend against these attacks is with punches and kicks, the following Qin Na techniques may also be used.

Qin Na means "seize and control," and it is one of the most effective ways of fighting at short range. In this section we will only introduce a few techniques useful against common grabbing attacks.

A. Defense against Wrist Grabs:
Technique #1:

There are four ways the opponent can grab your wrist or forearm. The first way is to grab your right wrist with his right hand (Figure 3-126). When this happens, lock his hand with your left hand (Figure 3-127) and circle your right hand upward (Figure 3-128). Turn your right hand forward and wrap his wrist with it,

Figure 3-127.

Figure 3-128.

and then push down to lock him in place (Figure 3-129). Then step your right leg back and press him down until his elbow touches the ground (Figure 3-130). When you lock his wrist, make sure that his elbow is lower than his wrist, otherwise he will be able to turn his body (Figures 3-131 and 3-132). If you start to lose control of him, immediately kick him in the groin with your right leg (Figure 3-133).

Technique #2:

If your opponent grabs your right wrist with his left hand (Figure 3-134), again lock his hand with your left hand, then circle your right hand upward and then downward to control him (Figures

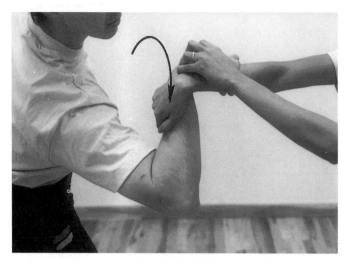

Figure 3-129.

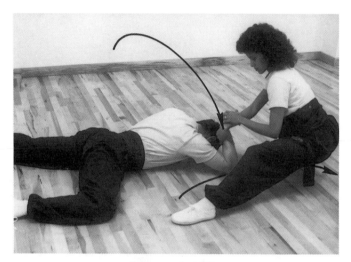

Figure 3-130.

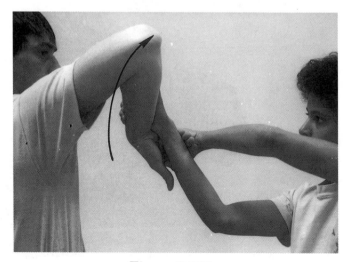

Figure 3-131.

Figure 3-132.

Figure 3-133.

3-135 and 3-136). Again, his elbow should be lower than his wrist in order to prevent him from turning. If you execute the technique correctly, you will not need too much power to control him. Press down on his wrist until his elbow touches the ground, and at the same time step your left leg back (Figure 3-137). If necessary, you may use your left leg to kick him (Figure 3-138).

Technique #3:
If your opponent grabs your right wrist with his left hand as shown in Figure 3-139, simply lower your right wrist and raise your right elbow, while at the same time grabbing and locking his hand with your

Figure 3-134.   Figure 3-135.

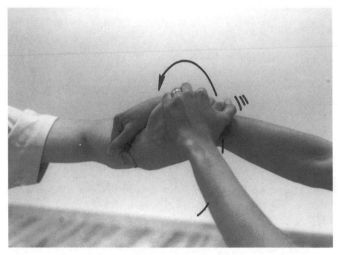

Figure 3-136.

left hand (Figure 3-140). Next, push his elbow down with your elbow. Immediately bend forward and to your right (Figure 3-141). You should keep pressing down until his right hand touches the ground.

Technique #4:

If your opponent grabs your right wrist with his right hand as shown in Figure 3-142, grab his right wrist with your left hand, and then push his elbow to your right with your left elbow while turning your body to your right (Figure 3-143). Immediately bend forward and lock his elbow until he is standing on his toes (Figure 3-144). If necessary, you may pop his elbow and shoulder out of joint.

B. Defense against Sleeve Grabs:

Figure 3-137.

Figure 3-138.

Technique #1:

If your opponent grabs your right sleeve with his right hand (Figure 3-145), grab his wrist with your right hand while turning your body to your right and using your left upper arm to push his elbow upward (Figure 3-146). Finally, use both of your arms to lock his elbow upward (Figure 3-147). Control him until he is standing on his toes.

Technique #2:

When he grabs your left sleeve with his right hand (Figure 3-148), grab his wrist with both hands (Figure 3-149), while at the same time circling your elbow over his elbow while turning your body to your right (Figure 3-150). Finally, press your elbow downward to immobilize him (Figure 3-151).

C. Defense against Shoulder Grabs:
Technique #1:

If your opponent grabs your right upper arm or shoulder with his right hand (Figure 3-152), turn to your right while grabbing his

-85-

Figure 3-139.

Figure 3-140.

Figure 3-141.

Figure 3-142.

Figure 3-143.

Figure 3-144.

Figure 3-145.

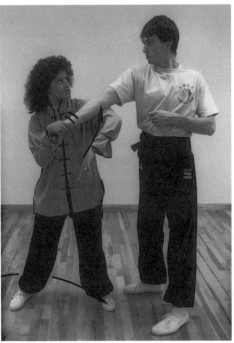

Figure 3-146.

Figure 3-147.

Figure 3-148.

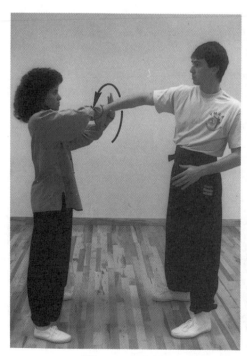

Figure 3-149.

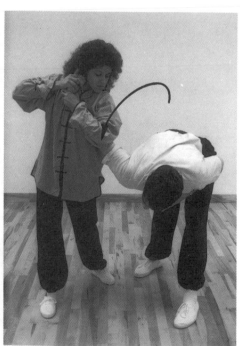

Figure 3-150.

Figure 3-151.

Figure 3-152.

Figure 3-153.

Figure 3-154.

wrist with your right hand (Figure 3-153). Then, immediately use your left shoulder to lock his right arm upward (Figure 3-154). You should control him until his heels are up.

Technique #2:

    If he is using his right hand to grab your left upper arm or

Figure 3-155.

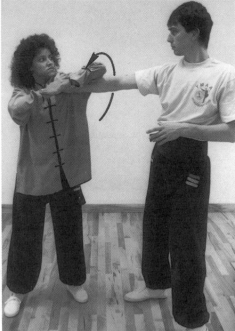

Figure 3-156.

Figure 3-157.

shoulder (Figure 3-155), first grab his hand tightly with your right hand while at the same time covering his right arm with your left arm (Figures 3-156 and 3-157). Then bend forward while controlling his wrist (Figure 3-158). His elbow should be lower than his wrist. For complete control, bend forward until his left hand touches the ground, otherwise, he can still punch your face with his left hand.

D. Defense against Chest Grabs:
Technique #1:

When your opponent grabs your chest with his right hand, if his palm is facing down (Figure 3-159) grab his hand with both of yours, and turn his hand to your right to an angle where you can control

Figure 3-158.

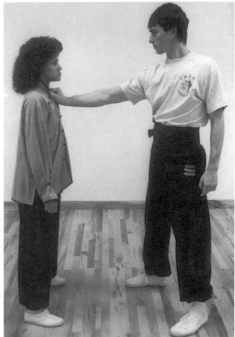

Figure 3-159.

Figure 3-160.

Figure 3-161.

him (Figure 3-160). Slide your left hand to his right elbow and press it downward (Figure 3-161). Then, continue to press your opponent's right elbow downward with your left hand and bend forward (Figure 3-162). This will lock his wrist into a painful position.

Technique #2:

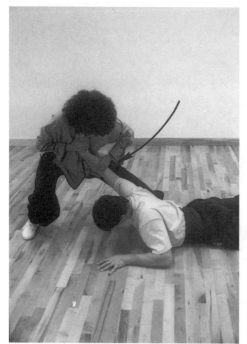

Figure 3-162.

Figure 3-163.

Figure 3-164.

Figure 3-165.

When your opponent grabs you with his palm facing upward (Figure 3-163), the previous technique will be difficult to use. Instead, grab his right wrist with your left hand, and push his elbow to your right with your left upper arm while turning your body (Figure 3-164). Finally, bend forward and lock his right arm behind your back (Figure 3-165). You should continue to bend forward until

Figure 3-166.

Figure 3-167.

his heels are up.

E.   Defense against Hair Grabs:
Technique #1:

If your hair has been grabbed and you cannot kick his groin or punch his face (Figure 3-166), immediately grab his wrist tightly with both hands, pull his body forward and downward while stepping your right leg backward (Figure 3-167). Next, step your right leg behind his right leg while twisting his wrist (Figure 3-168). Finally, lift your hands upward to lock him upward (Figure 3-169). Alternatively, you may step your left leg backward first and pull him

Figure 3-168.

Figure 3-169.

Figure 3-170.

down (Figure 3-170). Next. turn your body to your right while twisting his arm (Figure 3-171). Finally, pull him down to the ground (Figure 3-172).

F. Defense against Neck Grabs:
Technique #1:

If someone in front of you grabs your neck with both hands (Figure 3-173), the easiest way is to punch his nose (Figure 3-174) or kick his groin or shin. Otherwise, you may grab his right hand with your right hand while covering his right forearm with your left arm (Figures 3-175 and 3-176). Turn to your right while pressing his

Figure 3-171.

Figure 3-172.

elbow down with your left elbow, and bend forward (Figure 3-177).

Technique #2:

However, if someone grabs your neck from behind (Figure 3-178), immediately turn your head to the side to protect your throat while using both hands to pull his arm out (Figure 3-179). Use an elbow to strike his solar plexus while still holding on to his wrist (Figure 3-180), or use your heel to kick his foot, shin, or groin (Figure 3-181). You may also strike his groin (Figure 3-182). Once his attention is distracted, immediately grab his wrist with both hands and turn to control him (Figures 3-183 and 3-184).

Figure 3-173.

Figure 3-174.

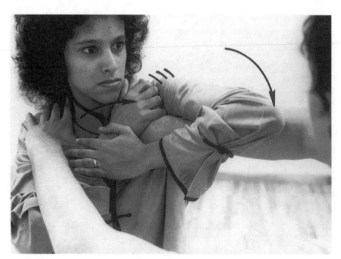

Figure 3-175.

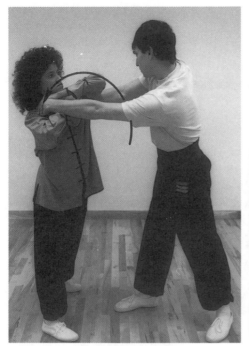

Figure 3-176.

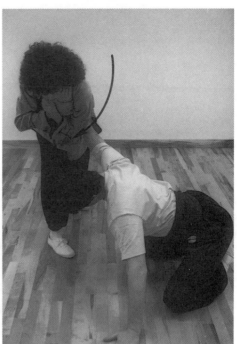

Figure 3-177.

Figure 3-178.

Figure 3-179.

Figure 3-180.

Figure 3-181.

Figure 3-182.

Figure 3-183.

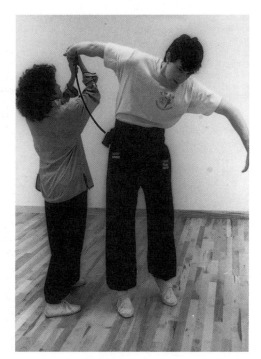

Figure 3-184.

Chapter 4
Defense Against Knife
Attack

4-1. Introduction

Defending against a knife attack is usually harder and much more dangerous than defending against a barehand attack, so speed is extremely important. You must also perform your techniques firmly and accurately.

At this point, I would like to remind you again that if your opponent has a gun and keeps a good distance away from you, then you should not try to fight back unless you are absolutely sure that your life is in danger. If it is only a question of money, then give it to him. A bullet is much faster than you are, and your life isn't worth the risk. However, if the opponent is quite a distance away from you, you may have a chance to run and find something to hide behind. If the distance is very short and you can reach the gun without stepping, then you may also have a chance to counter and disarm the opponent. However, you must be very proficient to do this. Otherwise, you are taking an enormous risk.

In the next section we will introduce some basic training for use against knife attacks. This will give you a foundation to understand the techniques described in the third section.

4-2. Basic Training

To defend against a knife attack, in addition to the basic training for speed, accuracy, and power which was introduced in the last chapter, you also need other specific drills.

When defending against a knife, distance, the angle at which you face the opponent, timing, and the accuracy of your interception are extremely important. Any mistake can get you hurt. In this section, therefore, we will focus on escaping from or intercepting an attack. It is best if you practice with a training partner, and still better if you have several partners so that you can get used to a

Figure 4-1.

Figure 4-2.

variety of body types and personalities.

Start by having your partner attack you with a rubber knife so that you can practice escaping from the attacks any way you can. Once you can do this easily, practice intercepting the attack by pushing the wrist or hand.

Once you have learned how to escape, have your partner attack you any way he likes while you practice avoiding the attack by changing the distance and angle to him. For example, if your partner stabs at you with his right hand, you can dodge backward (Figure 4-1), to his left (Figure 4-2), or to his right (Figure 4-3). Dodging backward is not as good as dodging to the side because the attacker can easily hop forward and continue his attack (Figure 4-4). In addition, if you keep dodging backward, you may be forced into a corner or against a wall. Dodging to the side gives you a chance to circle him or even enter his empty door for an attack.

Once you can escape easily, then you must learn how to intercept the attack. If you get attacked in an area where there is not

Figure 4-3.

Figure 4-4.

enough room to keep retreating or dodging, you will have to intercept the attack skillfully. If you know how to intercept, you will not
need too much space to defend yourself. To learn how to intercept a
knife attack, again have your partner attack you any way he likes
while you practice intercepting with your hands. How you intercept
an attack depends on the actual situation, and also on how your
opponent is holding the knife. For example, if your opponent thrusts
the knife at you with the tip of the knife pointing at you, you may
use your right hand to slap his right wrist while you are dodging to
his left (Figure 4-5). Alternatively, you may use your left hand to
slap his right wrist while dodging to his right (Figure 4-6).

Again, retreating backward is not as good as dodging to the
sides, because the opponent can hop forward faster than you can
retreat and stab you. Furthermore, if you only retreat backward,
you will find it difficult to get close enough to him to counterattack.
When you dodge to the side, however, it is much easier to close the
distance between you and your opponent (Figure 4-7).

Figure 4-5.

Figure 4-6.

Figure 4-7.

Figure 4-8.

Figure 4-9.

When your opponent, however, holds the knife with the blade projecting from the little finger side of his hand, his reach is relatively shorter, and his choice of techniques is also limited. For example, he can stab you (Figure 4-8) or slice you (Figure 4-9). Usually this grip is used only by professional martial artists who have trained how to use the knife in coordination with kicks and body movement. For untrained people, however, the first grip is easier and more common.

To intercept a stabbing attack with the knife held this way, step backward or dodge to the side, and at the same time cover his wrist with one hand (Figure 4-10). If he tries to slice you, you may use the same covering technique to prevent him from attacking you again (Figure 4-11). However, one of the best ways to defend against an attacker who is holding the knife this way is to kick him, since your leg is probably longer than his arm and knife (Figure 4-12). In fact, you should use your legs as much as possible. To practice, have your partner attack you any way he likes while using this grip. Practice

Figure 4-10.

Figure 4-11.

Figure 4-12.

Figure 4-13.

Figure 4-14.

stepping backward or to the sides while also kicking his shin, knee, abdomen, or groin (Figures 4-13 to 4-15).

Next, you should learn how to use a belt, clothes, or even shoes to intercept an attack. First have your partner attack you so that you can practice using an article of clothing to intercept. Hold the end of the article in one hand and wrap the material around your forearm (Figure 4-16). Practice intercepting with this arm until you can skillfully push the attack to the side (Figures 4-17 and 4-18) or downward (Figure 4-19).

You should then also learn how to use a belt to intercept an attack. Wrap an end of the belt around each hand (Figure 4-20). When your partner attacks, intercept with the center part of the belt. When you dodge to your left, have your right hand on top and your left hand on the bottom (Figure 4-21), and when you dodge to your right, have your left hand on the top and your right hand on the bottom (Figure 4-22). You can also push the attack downward

Figure 4-15.

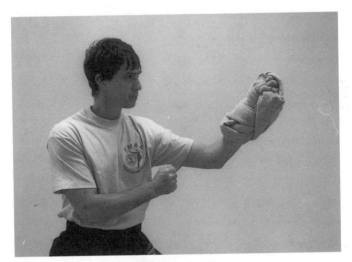

Figure 4-16.

Figure 4-17.

Figure 4-18.

Figure 4-19.

Figure 4-20.

Figure 4-21.

Figure 4-22.

(Figure 4-23). Once you have blocked the attack, you may be able to punch with either hand. An article of clothing can also be used to block this way.

Once you have mastered the footwork and dodging tactics, you should learn how to snap the belt. First practice holding the end with the buckle, and learn how to snap the belt so that it hits the target and bounces back quickly (Figure 4-24). Once you can do this comfortably, practice holding the belt by the other end and snapping the end with the buckle at the target. You can do a lot more damage to your opponent that way.

Finally, you can also practice intercepting with shoes. Put your hands inside the shoes to protect them (Figure 4-25), and then practice blocking your partners attacks without losing your shoes (Figure 4-26).

4-3. Techniques

In this section we will introduce techniques which use a belt,

Figure 4-23.

Figure 4-24.

Figure 4-25.

Figure 4-26.

Figure 4-27.

shoes, or an article of clothing, as well as barehand techniques. This should give you a lot of ideas to explore in your practice. Exactly what strategy and techniques you use will, of course, depend upon the actual situation.

1. Using a Belt:

Attacking with a belt can be a very effective defensive technique against someone coming at you with a knife. This is true even if you have only practiced for a few hours. If you are skillful, attack with the buckle end. If you are not very experienced, hold the buckle and snap the other end. This will eliminate the risk of your getting hit by the buckle when it bounces back.

Technique #1:

If your opponent is holding the knife in his right hand, circle to his left while snapping the belt at his eyes (Figure 4-27). Since the belt is longer than the knife, this will put your opponent into a defensive situation. Immediately after your strike, kick his shin or

Figure 4-28.

Figure 4-29.

groin (Figure 4-28).

Technique #2:
If your opponent is holding the knife in his left hand, circle to his right to get away from the knife. While moving to his side, snap the belt at his face (Figure 4-29), and immediately follow this up with a kick (Figure 4-30).

Technique #3:
If your belt is very light or not very strong, do not use it for snapping because it will not do the opponent much damage. If he is not afraid of the belt, there is a very good chance that he can grab it. Instead, wrap the belt around each hand and use the center area for blocking (Figure 4-31). Right after intercepting the attack, immediately kick your opponent (Figures 4-32 and 4-33). Alternatively, if you are fast and skillful, you may use the belt to catch the attacking arm with a circling, wrapping technique (Figure 4-34).

Figure 4-30.

Figure 4-31.

Figure 4-32.

Figure 4-33.

Figure 4-34.

2.   Using Clothes or Shoes:
Technique #1:
If you are not wearing a belt, take off your jacket or an article of clothing and wrap it around one of your arms and use that arm to intercept the attack. After the block, immediately punch the opponent's face (Figure 4-35) or kick his knee (Figure 4-36).

Technique #2:
Take off your shoes, put your hands in them, and use them to intercept the attack (Figure 4-37). Right after intercepting, immediately punch or kick your opponent (Figure 4-38).

Technique #3:
You may throw one of your shoes in the opponent's face to create an opportunity to attack (Figure 4-39). However, if the attack fails, you will have lost half of your protection.

3.   Using your Arms and/or Legs:

Figure 4-35.

Figure 4-36.

Figure 4-37.

You can defend yourself against a knife attack with only your arms and legs, but you should try this only as a last resort when you cannot find anything to use as a weapon, or when the situation is too urgent and you do not have the time to pick up anything. Unarmed defense against a knife attack requires not only speed and skill, but also accuracy in your interception and counterattack.

Technique #1:

The best and safest way to defend against a knife attack bare-handed is to avoid intercepting the attacking hand. You can do this by circling your opponent and always staying at the entrance to his empty door (Figure 4-40). This will prevent him from attacking you

Figure 4-38.

Figure 4-39.

Figure 4-40.

Figure 4-41.

Figure 4-42.

easily. If you can kick fast and powerfully, then when your opponent attacks you, dodge to his empty door and at the same time kick his shin, kneecap, or groin (Figure 4-41). After the kick, immediately punch his face (Figure 4-42). Remember to keep your kicks low so that he cannot easily cut your leg. If he does try to attack your leg, he will bring his face into range of your own attack. If he does this, immediately take the opportunity and punch his face.

Technique #2:

If you prefer using your hands to attack, then they have to be faster and more skillful than your legs. The reason for this is that, when you use your hands to block and attack, both of your hands are in range of his knife, and you can get cut easily on your hands and arms.

If you use your hands to counter the knife, you should wait for your opponent to attack first. If you attack first, your opponent can easily use the knife to cut your hands. When your opponent attacks,

Figure 4-43.

Figure 4-44.

use either hand to intercept at his wrist. If you intercept with your right hand, push his hand to your left (Figure 4-43) and immediately attack with your right hand to his face (Figure 4-44). You may also kick his shin, knee, or groin (Figure 4-45).

Technique #3:

However, if you intercept with your left hand, push or cover the attacking hand to your right (Figure 4-46) and immediately strike the opponent's face or throat with your left hand (Figure 4-47). You may also kick his knee or shin (Figure 4-48).

4.   Using Qin Na:

Using Qin Na against a knife attack is very dangerous unless you are quite proficient. Generally speaking, punching and kicking the opponent to injure him is easier than seizing and controlling him. Before you can us Qin Na efficiently, you must practice until you are very skillful, fast, and accurate in every technique.

The intercepting techniques you use vary, depending upon

Figure 4-45.

Figure 4-46.

Figure 4-47.

Figure 4-48.

Figure 4-49.

whether the opponent is holding the knife with the point on the thumb-side (point-out) (Figure 4-49) or on the little finger side of the hand (point-in or point-down) (Figure 4-50).

A. Techniques Against a Knife Held Point-out:
Technique #1:

If your opponent stabs at your chest, cover the attack with your left hand on his wrist while simultaneously clamping upward with your right hand (Figure 4-51). Turn both hands counterclockwise to twist his wrist (Figures 4-52 and 4-53), then press downward with both hands until his elbow touches the ground or he is lying on the ground (Figure 4-54). When you control him, the knife should be pointing at his face or neck. If necessary, you can move his hands so that he cuts or stabs himself with his own knife (Figure 4-55).

If you cannot control your opponent easily, immediately punch him in the nose with your right hand (Figure 4-56).

Figure 4-50.

Figure 4-51.

Figure 4-52.

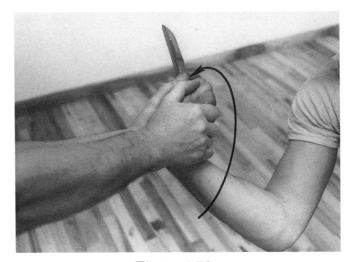

Figure 4-53.

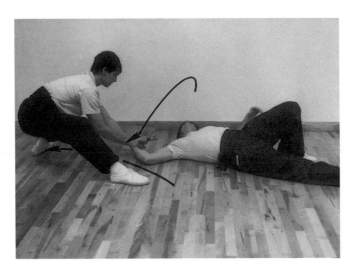

Figure 4-54.

Figure 4-55.

Figure 4-56.

Figure 4-57.

Technique #2:

If your opponent stabs your chest, cover the attack with your right hand and clamp his wrist with your left hand (Figure 4-57), then immediately turn your body to your right while moving your left elbow over his elbow to lock it under your armpit (Figure 4-58). Keep his arm straight and press downward with your shoulder while bending your left knee to the ground (Figure 4-59). Apply pressure until your opponent's face touches the ground.

If you find that you are losing control of his wrist, immediately kick his groin with your right leg (Figure 4-60).

Technique #3:

If your opponent stabs your chest, cover the attack with your left hand and clamp upward with your right hand (Figure 4-61). Move his forearm counterclockwise while locking his wrist with your left hand (Figures 4-62 and 4-63). Finally, push your opponent's elbow upward with your right hand and lock him in place (Figure 4-64). When you are controlling your opponent, keep the knife point-

Figure 4-58.

Figure 4-59.

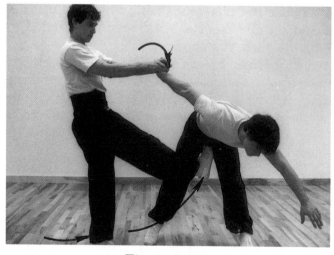

Figure 4-60.

Figure 4-61.

Figure 4-62.

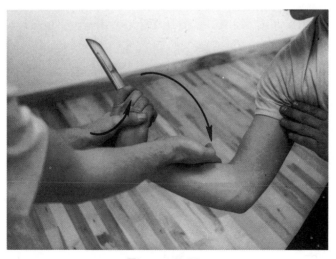

Figure 4-63.

Figure 4-64.

Figure 4-65.

ing at his neck so that you can cut or stab him with it.

While you are doing this technique, you may kick the back of his right knee with your right leg to bring him down (Figure 4-65).

Technique #4:

If your opponent stabs at you, cover his attack with your right hand and clamp upward with your left hand (Figure 4-66). Circle his arm to your right while holding on tightly to his wrist with both hands (Figure 4-67), and then press down on his wrist to push him down (Figure 4-68).

Right after you have turned his hand to your right, you may immediately strike his throat with your forearm (Figure 4-69).

Technique #5:

If your opponent stabs at your chest with his right hand, first cover the attack with your right hand while clamping upward with your left hand (Figure 4-70). Immediately move your right hand to his elbow and hook it (Figure 4-71). If you use the leverage of both

Figure 4-66.

Figure 4-67.

Figure 4-68.

Figure 4-69.

Figure 4-70.

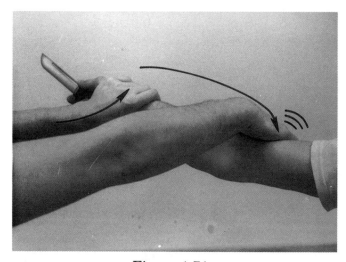

Figure 4-71.

Figure 4-72.

Figure 4-73.

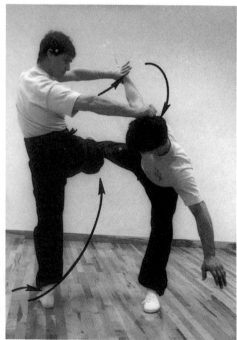

Figure 4-74.

hands, you can break his elbow very easily or bring him down (Figure 4-72).

You may also move your right hand along his arm to grab his hair and pull his head downward so that you can knee his face, chest, or groin (Figure 4-73). Alternatively, you may sweep his right leg and make him fall (Figure 4-74). Once you have locked his arm, there are many other techniques which you may use.

Technique #6:

When your opponent stabs at you with the knife in his right hand, you may again use your right hand to cover his wrist (Figure 4-75). Then grab his wrist with your left hand and grab his throat with your

Figure 4-75.

Figure 4-76.

right hand while stepping your right leg behind his right leg (Figure 4-76). Sweep your right leg backward while pressing your right arm downward against his throat to make him fall (Figure 4-77).

Right after your left hand has immobilized his right arm, you may use your right hand to strike his temple or poke his eyes, or you may strike him in the chest with your elbow (Figure 4-78).

Technique #7:

When your opponent stabs you, dodge slightly to your right while using your left hand to repel his wrist (Figure 4-79). Right after the repelling, immediately grab his wrist with your left hand while placing your right forearm under his elbow to lock him upward (Figure 4-80). If you use the leverage of your both hands, you can easily break his elbow.

Technique #8:

Similar in theory to the previous technique, you may also dodge slightly to your left and repel the attack with your right hand

Figure 4-77.

Figure 4-78.

Figure 4-79.

Figure 4-80.

Figure 4-81.

(Figure 4-81). Then grab his wrist with your right hand while stepping your left leg behind him and locking his elbow upward with your left arm (Figure 4-82). You may break his elbow from this position if necessary. If you feel that your arm is too weak to lock his elbow, you may use your shoulder instead (Figure 4-83). It is also very easy for you to strike his lower ribs with your left elbow (Figure 4-84).

Technique #9:
If your opponent stabs to your lower body, you may repel the attack to your right with your left forearm while grabbing his wrist with your right hand (Figure 4-85). Circle your left arm counter-clockwise upward and then downward (Figures 4-86 and 4-87), and lock his wrist and elbow in position (Figure 4-88). Alternatively, right after you have intercepted the attack and grabbed his wrist (Figure 4-89), you may step back with your right leg (Figure 4-90) and bring your opponent to the ground in an arc (Figure 4-91). You

Figure 4-82.

Figure 4-83.

Figure 4-84.

have to use the leverage of both arms to move him easily.

Technique #10:

If your opponent stabs to your lower body, intercept the attack with your right arm and grab his wrist with your left hand (Figure 4-92). Immediately move your right arm to his elbow and press

Figure 4-85.

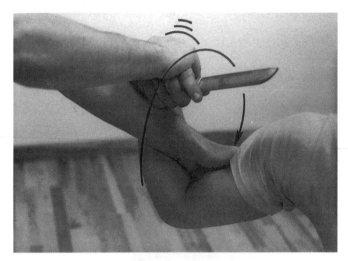

Figure 4-86.

Figure 4-87.

Figure 4-88.

Figure 4-89.

Figure 4-90.

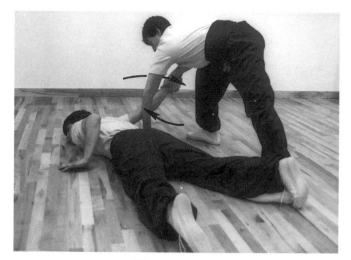

Figure 4-91.

Figure 4-92.

Figure 4-93.

Figure 4-94.

upward to lock it in place (Figure 4-93). If necessary, you can easily break his elbow.

As with the previous techniques, you have a number of options for punching or kicking your opponent.

B. Techniques Against a Knife Held Point-in or Point-down:

When your opponent holds his knife with the point on the little finger side of the hand, you should only use covering techniques to intercept (Figure 4-94). If you intercept by repelling, your forearm can be cut easily (Figure 4-95).

Technique #11:

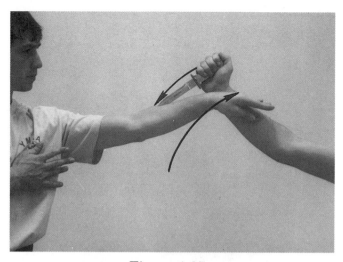

Figure 4-95.

Figure 4-96.

If your opponent stabs at you with the knife in his right hand, cover his wrist with your left hand while clamping upward with your right hand (Figure 4-96). Twist and pull his wrist until his elbow touches the ground or until he is lying on the ground (Figures 4-97 and 4-98).

Technique #12:

This is similar in theory to the last technique. Cover the attack with your right hand while clamping upward with your left hand (Figure 4-99). Twist his wrist and press downward until his face touches the floor (Figures 4-100 and 4-101).

Technique #13:

If your opponent stabs at your chest, cover the attack with your left hand while clamping upward with your right hand (Figure 4-102). Move his forearm counterclockwise while locking his wrist with your left hand (Figure 4-103). Then push his elbow upward with your right hand and lock him in position (Figures 4-104 and 4-105). When you

Figure 4-97.

Figure 4-98.

Figure 4-99.

Figure 4-100.

Figure 4-101.

Figure 4-102.

Figure 4-103.

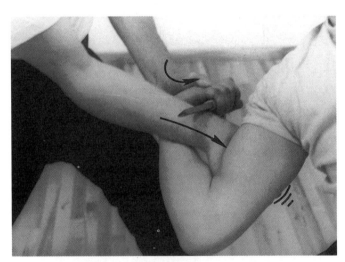

Figure 4-104.

Figure 4-105.

Figure 4-106.

Figure 4-107.

have him controlled, the knife should be pointing at his neck so that you can cut or stab him with it.

Technique #14:
When your opponent stabs at your chest, cover his wrist with your left hand while clamping upward with your right hand (Figure 4-106). Then grab his wrist with your right hand while circling your left arm around his neck (Figure 4-107). Of course, you may may instead use your left arm to attack his face or neck (Figure 4-108).

Technique #15:
When your opponent stabs at your chest, cover his wrist with

Figure 4-108.

Figure 4-109.

your left hand while clamping upward with your right hand (Figure 4-109). Turn your body to your right while pushing upward with your elbow (Figure 4-110). You may also turn your body completely to your rear while moving your legs together, and use your back to generate the pressure (Figure 4-111).

You can see that there are fewer Qin Na techniques which can be used when the knife is held point-in or point-down than when it is held point-out. However, there is also only a limited number of ways in which the opponent can attack you when he is holding the knife this way. In addition, when he holds the knife this way, his range is more limited. It is therefore safer and more effective for you to use kicks.

Figure 4-110.   Figure 4-111.

The Chinese martial arts have many more Qin Na techniques for use against knife attacks. Remember, however, that **IT IS BETTER TO MASTER A FEW TECHNIQUES THAN TO LEARN MANY TECHNIQUES POORLY**. In fact, if you master all of the techniques we have shown, you will find that you can discover or create many other techniques by yourself.

Chapter 5
Conclusion

The techniques and strategies which we have discussed in this book are actually only a tiny portion of the White Crane and Long Fist systems. We have selected those we deem most practical and easiest for beginners to learn. If you practice an hour each day, you should be able to master all of the techniques within six months. If you chose to learn a whole martial system, it would take you at least ten years to acquire its essence.

This book has been written for those people who would like to learn how to defend themselves in a relatively short period of time. If, at some future date, you choose to begin serious study in a martial school, you will find that the training in this book has given you a good foundation.

Finally, I would like to re-emphasize a very important fact. A theory is only a theory and a technique is only a technique. They remain dead unless you know how to bring them to life and use them skillfully. If someone actually attacks you, you will not have any time to think, so all your reactions must come very naturally and automatically. It is just like when you are driving: if an urgent situation arises, you must be able to negotiate it without thought or hesitation.

Appendix A
Glossary of Chinese Terms

Ba Ji: 八极

Eight Extremities or Eight Tactics. A style of Changquan (Long Fist). The entire name is Kai Men Ba Ji Quan (Opening Gate Eight Extremities Fist). This style is said to have been created by the first emperor of the Ming Dynasty, Zhu Yuan-Zhang. It has also been said that this style was revealed to the public by the Jiao Zuo Yue Shan Temple, Henan. It has therefore also been called Yue Shan Ba Ji (Yue Mountain Eight Extremities). This style is popular in northern China.

Bai He: 白鶴

White Crane. A style of Chinese martial arts.

Cha Quan: 查拳

Cha's Fist or Fork Fist. A northern Chinese martial style which originated in Xi Yu (West Territory), China. It is said that this style was created by a Muslim named Cha Shang-Yi (or Cha Mi-Er) during the Ming dynasty (1368-1644 A.D.). This style includes ten practice routines (or sequences). It is also said that this style has adopted the fighting characteristics of five animals: dragon, tiger, snake, crane, and monkey.

Chang Ju: 長距

Long range. In Chinese martial arts, the distance at which neither opponent can reach the other with a punch or kick without stepping or hopping forward.

Changquan (Chang Chuan): 長拳

Long fist/style/sequence. A style of Northern Chinese Gongfu which specializes in kicking and long range fighting. The term Changquan has also been used to refer to Taijiquan.

Cuo Jiao: 戳脚

Literally, "stamp foot." A Chinese northern martial style specializing in leg techniques.

Da Mo: 達摩

The Indian Buddhist monk who is credited with creating the Yi

Jin Jing and Xi Sui Jing while at the Shaolin monastery. His last name was Sardili, and he was also known as Bodhidarma. He was once the prince of a small tribe in southern India.

Dan Tian: 丹田

Literally: Field of Elixir. Locations in the body which are able to store and generate Qi (elixir) in the body. The Upper, Middle, and Lower Dan Tians are located respectively between the eyebrows, at the solar plexus, and a few inches below the navel.

Di Tang: 地躺

Literally "Ground Lying." A style of Chinese martial arts which specializes in fighting from the ground. This style was described in General Qi Ji-Guang's book "Ji Xiao Xin Shu" (The New Book of Recorded Effectiveness) during the Ming dynasty (1522 A.D.). Today, this style is divided into northern and southern styles.

Dian Xue: 點穴

Dian means "to point and exert pressure" and Xue means "the cavities." Dian Xue refers to those Qin Na techniques which specialize in attacking acupuncture cavities to immobilize or kill an opponent.

Duan Ju: 短距

Short range. The distance between two fighters where either one can reach the other with his hands. This fighting range is the most urgent and dangerous.

Fan Zi: 翻子

Fluttering or Flying. A long range Northern fighting style, also classified as Changquan. It is also called "Ba Shan Fan" (Eight Dodge Fluttering) or simply "Fan Quan" (Fluttering Fist). This style was also recorded in General Qi Ji Guang's book "Ji Xiao Xin Shu" (The New Book of Recording Efficiency). It is believed that this style was originally created in the Shaolin Temple in Henan. It is very popular in northern China.

Fei He: 飛鶴

Flying Crane. A sub-style of the White Crane system which specializes in jumping to dodge and attack.

Fujian: 福建

A province in the southeast corner of China.

Gongfu (Kung Fu): 功夫

Literally: energy-time. Any study, learning, or practice which requires a lot of patience, energy, and time to complete. Since practicing Chinese martial arts requires a great deal of time and energy, Chinese martial arts are commonly called Gongfu.

Guo Ming Dang: 國民黨

The political party created by Dr. Sun Yat-Sen (1866-1925 A.D.). After World War II, after the victory of the Chinese communists this party retreated to Taiwan under the leadership of Chiang Kai-Shek.

Guoshu: 國術

Literally: national techniques. Another name for Chinese martial arts. First used by President Chiang Kai-Shek in 1926 at the founding of the Nanking Central Guoshu Institute.

Heng Xin: 恒心

Patience. One of the martial moralities which are taught to Chinese martial artists.

Hsing Yi Chuan: 形意拳

See: Xingyiquan.

Hua Quan: 華拳

Brilliant Fist. A northern Chinese martial style (Changquan). This style was created in Xi Yu (West Mountain), it is therefore also called "Xi Yu Hua Quan" (Hua Fist of West Mountain). It is so named because it emphasizes the cultivation of the three Brilliancies (San Hua), essence (Jing), internal energy (Qi), and spirit (Shen), and uniting them into one (San Hua Guan Yi).

Jing: 劲

A power in Chinese martial arts which is derived from muscles which have been energized by Qi to their maximum potential.

Kung Fu: 功夫

See: Gongfu.

Liu He: 六合

Six Combination (Fist). A branch of the Wei Tuo style, which is named after a Buddhist god whose job is to keep away evil and to guard temples. Liu He is a major branch of the martial arts in the Shaolin Temple in Henan, and it combines external and internal training. The six combinations unite the three internal elements: essence (Jing), internal energy (Qi), and spirit (Shen), and the three external elements: hands, eyes, and body. Its applications emphasize the combination of Xin (emotional mind) and Yi (wisdom mind), Yi and Qi, and Qi and Li (muscular power). The keys to its training are the combination of the body and hands, hands and feet, and feet and hips.

Mei Hua: 梅花

Plum Flower Fist. A northern style of Chinese martial arts (Changquan). It is also called "Mei Hua Zhuang" (Plum Flower Post) and emphasizes training while standing on posts arranged in the pattern of a plum flower.

Ming He: 鳴鶴

Shouting Crane. A branch of the Southern White Crane style which emphasizes Qi development, it imitates the cries of a fighting crane.

Pi Gua: 劈挂

A northern Chinese martial style developed before the Ming dynasty.

Qi: 氣

The general definition of Qi is: universal energy, including heat, light, and electromagnetic energy. A narrower definition of Qi refers to the energy circulating in human or animal bodies.

Qian Long Xia Jiang Nan: 乾隆下江南

Emperor Qian Long visits South of the River. A well known novel written during the Qing dynasty. The author is unknown. The background of this story contains a wealth of accurate historical information.

Qian Xu: 謙虛

Humility. One of the martial moralities.

Qigong (Chi Kung): 氣功

Gong means Gongfu (lit. energy-time). Therefore, Qigong means study, research, and/or practices related to Qi.

Qin Na (Chin Na): 擒拿

Literally, grab control. A type of Chinese Gongfu which emphasizes grabbing techniques to control the opponent's joints in conjunction with attacking certain acupuncture cavities.

Ren Nai: 忍耐

Endurance. One of the martial moralities.

Shaolin: 少林

A Buddhist temple in Henan province, famous for its martial arts.

Shaolin Yan Yi: 少林演義

The Historical Drama of Shaolin. This well known novel, written by Shao Yu-Sheng during the Qing dynasty, is a source of historical information.

Shi He: 食鶴

Eating Crane, a branch of the southern White Crane martial style which emphasizes attacking with the "beak."

Su He: 宿鶴

See: Zong He.

Taijiquan (Tai Chi Chuan): 太极拳

Great Ultimate Fist. A style of Chinese internal martial arts which emphasizes the cultivation of internal Qi. The creation of Taijiquan during the Chinese Song dynasty (960-1206 A.D.) is credited to Zhang San-Feng.

Taizuquan: 太祖拳

A style of Chinese martial arts which is said to have been created by Song Taizu, founder of the Song dynasty.

Tang Lang: 螳蜋

Praying Mantis. A well known northern Chinese martial style (Changquan). This style is said to have been created by Wang Lang during the Ming dynasty. He is believed to have learned his martial arts at the Shaolin Temple.

Tong Bei Quan: 通背拳

Through the Back Fist. Also called "Tong Bi Quan" (Through the Arm Fist). A martial style whose techniques imitate the motions of an ape's long arms. This style is said to have been created in ancient times by a man named Bai Yuan Dao Ren (White Ape Daoist).

Tui Na: 推拿

Literally: push grab. Tui Na is one of the traditional Chinese massage styles which specializes in using pushing and grabbing to adjust abnormal Qi circulation and cure sicknesses.

Wai Dan: 外丹

External elixir. External Qigong exercises in which a practitioner will build up his Qi in his limbs and then lead it into the center of the body for nourishment.

Wude: 武德

Martial Morality.

Wushu: 武術

Literally: martial techniques. A common name for the Chinese martial arts. Many other terms are used, including: Wuyi (martial arts), Wugong (martial Gongfu), Guoshu (national techniques), and Gongfu (energy-time). Because Wushu has been modified in mainland China over the past forty years into gymnastic martial performance, many traditional Chinese martial artists have given up this name in order to avoid confusing modern Wushu with traditional Wushu. Recently, mainland China has attempted to bring modern Wushu back toward its traditional training and practice.

Xi Sui Jing: 洗髓經

Literally: Washing Marrow Classic, usually translated Marrow Washing Classic. A Qigong training which specializes in leading Qi to the marrow to cleanse it. It is believed that Xi Sui Jing training is the key to longevity and reaching spiritual enlightenment.

Xin: 心

Literally: Heart. Refers to the emotional mind.

Xin Yong: 信用

Trust. One of the martial moralities.

Xingyiquan (Hsing Yi Chuan): 形意拳

Literally: Shape-mind Fist. An internal style of Gongfu in which the mind or thinking determines the shape or movement of the body. Creation of the style is attributed to Marshal Yue Fei.

Yan Qing: 燕青

A personal name which is also the name of a northern Chinese martial style (Changquan). Yan Qing is considered a sub-style of the Cuo Jiao style, which emphasizes attacking the upper body.

Yi: 意

Mind. Specifically, the mind which is generated by clear thinking and judgement, and which is able to make you calm, peaceful, and wise.

Yi Jin Jing: 易筋經

Literally: changing muscle/tendon classic, usually called The Muscle/Tendon Changing Classic. Credited to Da Mo around 550 A.D., this work discusses Wai Dan Qigong training for strengthening the physical body.

Yi Li: 毅力

Perseverance. One of the martial moralities.

Yi Zhi: 意志

Persistance. One of the martial moralities.

Ying Zhua: 鷹爪

Eagle claw style. A style of Chinese martial arts.

Yong Gan: 勇敢

Bravery. One of the martial moralities.

Zhan He: 顫鶴

Trembling Crane. Also called "Zong He" (Ancestial Crane), or "Su He" (Sleeping Crane), a branch of the southern White Crane martial style. This school emphasizes facing aggression with calmness, and utilizes the crane's shaking power. It is also called ancestral crane because it is believed to carry most of the original essence of the Crane style.

Zheng Yi: 正義

Righteousness. One of the martial moralities.

Zhong Cheng: 忠誠

Loyalty. One of the martial moralities.

Zhong Ju: 中距

Middle range. The distance between two fighters where they can reach each other with kicks but not with hands.

Zong He: 宗鶴

See: Zhan He.

Zun Jing: 尊敬

Respect. One of the martial moralities.

Appendix B
Translation of Chinese Terms

少林　Shaolin
白鶴　Bai He
長拳　Changquan (Chang Chuan)
功夫　Kung Fu (Gongfu)
吳文慶　Wen-Ching Wu
楊俊敏　Yang Jwing-Ming
新竹縣　Xin Zhu Xian
臺灣　Taiwan
武術　Wushu
功夫　Gongfu (Kung Fu)
曾金灶　Cheng Gin-Gsao
太祖拳　Taizuquan
金紹峰　Jin Shao-Feng
擒拿　Qin Na (Chin Na)
推拿　Tui Na
點穴　Dian Xue
太極拳　Taijiquan (Tai Chi Chuan)
高濤　Kao Tao
李茂清　Li Mao-Ching
陳威伸　Wilson Chen
臺北　Taipei
韓慶堂　Han Ching-Tan
張詳三　Chang Xiang-San
太極　Taiji
氣功　Qigong
淡江學院　Tamkang College
長拳　Chang Chuan
國術　Guoshu

勁　Jing
形意拳　Hsing Yi Chuan
連步拳　Lien Bu Chuan
功力拳　Gung Li Chuan
外丹氣功　Wai Dan Chi Kung
國民黨　Guo Ming Dang
蔣介石　Chiang Kai-Shek

Chapter 1
武德　Wude
心　Xin
意　Yi
謙虛　Qian Xu
尊敬　Zun Jing
麗麗　Li-Li
黃　Huang
正義　Zheng Yi
趙　Zhao
秦　Qin
廉頗　Lian Bo
藺相如　Lin Xiang-Ru
晉　Jin
祁奚　Qi Xi
晉悼公　Duke Dao
解狐　Xie Hu
祈午　Qi Wu
信用　Xin Yong
周幽王　Emperor You
褒　Bao
褒姒　Bao Si
申后　Lady Shen

-152-

王朗　Wang Lang
白猿道人　Bai Yuan Dao Ren
武藝　Wuyi
武功　Wugong

INDEX

NOTES

Books & Videos from YMAA

YMAA Publication Center Books

B005R. QIGONG FOR HEALTH AND MARTIAL ARTS—Exercises and Meditation
B006. NORTHERN SHAOLIN SWORD
B007R. TAI CHI THEORY & MARTIAL POWER—Advanced Yang Style (formerly Advanced Yang Style Tai Chi Chuan, v.1)
B008R. TAI CHI CHUAN MARTIAL APPLICATIONS—Advanced Yang Style (formerly Advanced Yang Style Tai Chi Chuan, v.2)
B009. ANALYSIS OF SHAOLIN CHIN NA—Instructor's Manual for all Martial Styles
B010R. EIGHT SIMPLE QIGONG EXERCISES FOR HEALTH—The Eight Pieces of Brocade
B011R. THE ROOT OF CHINESE QIGONG—Secrets for Health, Longevity, & Enlightenment
B012. MUSCLE/TENDON CHANGING AND MARROW/BRAIN WASHING CHI KUNG—The Secret of Youth
B013. HSING YI CHUAN—Theory and Applications
B014R. THE ESSENCE OF TAIJI QIGONG—The Internal Foundation of Taijiquan
B015R. ARTHRITIS—The Chinese Way of Healing and Prevention (formerly Qigong for Arthritis)
B016. CHINESE QIGONG MASSAGE—General Massage
B017R. HOW TO DEFEND YOURSELF—Effective & Practical Martial Arts Strategies
B018. THE TAO OF BIOENERGETICS—East–West
B019R. TAI CHI CHUAN—24 & 48 Postures with Martial Applications (formerly Simplified Tai Chi Chuan)
B020. BAGUAZHANG—Emei Baguazhang
B021. COMPREHENSIVE APPLICATIONS OF SHAOLIN CHIN NA—The Practical Defense of Chinese Seizing Arts for All Styles
B022. TAIJI CHIN NA—The Seizing Art of Taijiquan
B023. PROFESSIONAL BUDO—Ethics, Chivalry, and the Samurai Code
B024. SONG OF A WATER DRAGON—Biography of He Yi An
B025. THE ESSENCE OF SHAOLIN WHITE CRANE—Martial Power and Qigong
B026. OPENINGS—A Zen Joke Guide for Serious Problem Solving
B027. WISDOM'S WAY—101 Tales of Chinese Wit
B028. CHINESE FAST WRESTLING FOR FIGHTING—The Art of San Shou Kuai Jiao
B029. CHINESE FITNESS—A Mind/Body Approach
B030. BACK PAIN—Chinese Qigong for Healing and Prevention
B031. 108 INSIGHTS INTO TAI CHI CHUAN—A String of Pearls
B032. THE TAI CHI BOOK—Refining and Enjoying a Lifetime of Practice
B033. THE MARTIAL ARTS ATHLETE—Mental and Physical Conditioning for Peak Performance

YMAA Publication Center Videotapes

T001. YANG STYLE TAI CHI CHUAN— and Its Applications
T002. SHAOLIN LONG FIST KUNG FU—Lien Bu Chuan and Its Applications
T003. SHAOLIN LONG FIST KUNG FU—Gung Li Chuan and Its Applications
T004. ANALYSIS OF SHAOLIN CHIN NA
T005. EIGHT SIMPLE QIGONG EXERCISES FOR HEALTH—The Eight Pieces of Brocade
T006. CHI KUNG FOR TAI CHI CHUAN
T007. ARTHRITIS—The Chinese Way of Healing and Prevention
T008. CHINESE QIGONG MASSAGE—Self Massage
T009. CHINESE QIGONG MASSAGE—With a Partner
T010. HOW TO DEFEND YOURSELF 1—Unarmed Attack
T011. HOW TO DEFEND YOURSELF 2—Knife Attack
T012. COMPREHENSIVE APPLICATIONS OF SHAOLIN CHIN NA 1
T013. COMPREHENSIVE APPLICATIONS OF SHAOLIN CHIN NA 2
T014. SHAOLIN LONG FIST KUNG FU—Yi Lu Mai Fu & Er Lu Mai Fu and Their Applications
T015. SHAOLIN LONG FIST KUNG FU—Shi Zi Tang and Its Applications
T016. TAIJI CHIN NA
T017. EMEI BAGUAZHANG 1—Basic Training, Qigong, Eight Palms, & Their Applications
T018. EMEI BAGUAZHANG 2—Swimming Body & Its Applications
T019. EMEI BAGUAZHANG 3—Bagua Deer Hook Sword & Its Applications
T020. XINGYIQUAN—The Twelve Animal Patterns & Their Applications
T021. SIMPLIFIED TAI CHI CHUAN—Simplified 24 Postures & Standard 48 Postures
T022. SUN STYLE TAIJIQUAN—With Applications
T023. WU STYLE TAIJIQUAN—With Applications
T024. TAI CHI CHUAN & APPLICATIONS—Simplified 24 Postures with Applications & Standard 48 Postures
T025. SHAOLIN LONG FIST KUNG FU—Xiao Hu Yuan (Roaring Tiger Fist) and Its Applications
T026. WHITE CRANE HARD QIGONG—The Essence of Shaolin White Crane
T027. WHITE CRANE SOFT QIGONG—The Essence of Shaolin White Crane
T028. BACK PAIN—Chinese Qigong for Healing & Prevention
T029. THE SCIENTIFIC FOUNDATION OF CHINESE QIGONG—A Lecture by Dr. Yang, Jwing-Ming

YMAA Publication Center 楊氏東方文化出版中心

38 Hyde Park Avenue • Jamaica Plain, MA 02130
1-800-669-8892 • email: ymaa@aol.com